Beyond the Headlines

Gordon Thiessen

Cross Training Publishing

BEYOND THE HEADLINES

Gordon Thiessen, Beyond the Headlines

ISBN 1-887002-38-3

Cross Training Publishing
220 West Third Street - Second Floor
Grand Island, NE 68801
(308) 384-5762

This book is manufactured in the United States of America.

Library of Congress Cataloging in Publication Data in Progress.

Published by Cross Training Publishing
220 West Third Street - Second Floor
Grand Island, NE 68801
1-800-430-8588

Introduction

Jesus often taught by using parables and stories. He used settings and people that were familiar to his listeners. His stories related truth to the lives of those he taught.

Today, many of us relate to sports and the athletes who play them. While Jesus used parables and stories that related to his generation, my hope is that you will find the following sports headlines and devotions easy to relate to and apply to your life.

Beyond the Headlines combines the issues and lessons taught in sports with a biblical perspective. Sports can teach us a lot of important lessons about life, but only when we understand it from God's perspective. Each devotion analyzes current sports headlines in light of Scripture. Hopefully, you'll find this dose of inspiration and perspiration helpful in your understanding of God's Word.

Jordan never lost zest for basketball

It was just another Sunday in the Arizona Fall League, just another pick-up game with that light-hitting outfielder who drove all the fancy cars. One of the Orioles prospects said, "The first game, he was lolly-gagging. He wasn't really doing much . . . but when we beat them, he got mad." How mad? Well, in the next game, Zaun had an open layup—or so he thought, "He came out of nowhere and swatted it into the stands where the wives were sitting—a big-time swat," Zaun said. Jordan being Jordan, he didn't leave it at just that. "Go tell your grandkids about that one," he said. Someone find Zaun a lawyer—he deserves a share of the proceeds from Jordan's return, along with all the other prospects that His Airness dunked on in Arizona. The day Michael Jordan returned to the NBA, he said the pickup games against the minor leaguers rekindled his desire to play basketball.

Jordan isn't the only athlete that retired and later had second thoughts. In fact, sports history has many former stars who tried to return to greatness, once they had discovered that they had not lost their zest for playing their sport. Although most end in disappointment, like tennis star Bjorn Borg, few, like boxing great George Foreman, are able to reclaim some, if not all, their former greatness. With Jordan there has never been any question about him losing his ability due to age, but only a question about his desire to play the game. And now, that question has been answered with a resounding–Yes! Following his 55-point game shortly after his return to the NBA, there were few doubters in the crowd.

While our zest for sports may be important, it's not nearly as important as the enthusiasm needed to serve our God. Here is how the Bible describes one church's lack of enthusiasm, "I know your deeds, that you are neither cold nor hot. I wish you were either one or the other! So, because you are lukewarm–neither hot nor cold– I am about to spit you out of my mouth. You say, 'I am rich: I have acquired wealth and do not need a thing. "But you do not realize that you are wretched, pitiful, poor, blind and naked" (Rev. 3:15-17).

The Apostle John was chewing out the Church in Laodicea in

this passage because they had lost their zest to serve God. Laodicea was a wealthy city known for its banking and industry. But despite its great wealth, they had a problem with their water supply. The aqueduct that was built to bring water to the city from the hot springs didn't work properly. By the time the water reached the city, it was neither hot nor refreshingly cool–only lukewarm. John's point was: the city had become as bland about their faith as the water that came into the city.

Are you hot or cold, when it comes to serving God? Is your faith lukewarm? Think about it when you drink lukewarm water–yuck! Do you remember the practices or games when you were dying to take a drink of water? Lukewarm water just didn't cut it. And neither does the faith of someone who is a halfhearted, in-name-only Christian who relies on his or her own talent and ability.

How can we maintain our zest for the faith?

• **Don't follow God halfway.** Commit yourself to letting God rekindle your faith and get you into the game. If you find yourself following God halfway, ask yourself, "How does my level of earthly wealth affect my spiritual desire?" Earthly wealth had become so important to the Laodiceans that what they could see and buy had become more important to them than the spiritual wealth that is unseen and eternal. Let me put it this way, if a major league baseball player, becomes more focused on salary negotiations than glorifying God–he will begin to lose his zest for serving Him. The riches that count, are the riches that are in Christ.

• **Decide to take a stand for your faith.** If you don't do anything for God, the tendency is to become lazy and indifferent toward your faith. Here is advice from the Apostle Paul about taking a stand for God, "Therefore, my dear brothers, stand firm. Let nothing move you. Always give yourselves fully to the work of the Lord, because you know that your labor in the Lord is not in vain" (1 Corinthians 15:58).

God doesn't want someone going half-speed for Him, anymore than a coach wants his team to play a game at half-speed. Don't hold back–you've got every reason to be fired up to serve God!

Bo Jackson 'Fading Into the Woodwork'

This wasn't the way it was supposed to end for Vincent Edward Jackson, the most famous Jackson not named Michael or Reggie. This Jackson was a sports legend who threatened to last forever. Jackson himself said, "I promise you that Bo Jackson, the jock, has definitely faded into the woodwork."

We all knew his day would come. Even his prime time commercials and endorsements had already begun to fade several years ago. But even then, it seemed like Bo knew he would somehow be back for another year. It didn't matter that he had an artificial hip–five to six major league teams still called during the baseball strike for his services. When Jackson was tackled several years ago and it ended his NFL career, we all hoped the "superman" would simply turn his talents to baseball full time and that he would show the sportsworld that he could endure anything.

Listen to what the Bible has to say about things that fade away . . . "'The brother in humble circumstances ought to take pride in his high position. But the one who is rich should take pride in his low position, because he will pass away like a wild flower. For the sun rises with scorching heat and withers the plant; its blossom falls and its beauty is destroyed. In the same ways the rich man will fade away even while he goes about his business" (James 1:9-11).

Do you spend too much time thinking about things that will fade? The Bible teaches that social status, material wealth and power mean nothing to God. While this world may be impressed by each of these areas and even honor us for them, each will fade. Whether it's Bo Jackson or Michael Jordan, everyone's accomplishments will someday mean very little to future sports fans. It seems impossible doesn't it?

It's been said that few people on their death bed will be glad they spent extra time working at the office. Instead, most will wish they spent more time investing in the lives of others or with developing their relationship with God. How can you begin to spend less time on things that fade and more time on things that last?

• **Decide what is really important in life.** You can start by defining what success is from God's perspective. Don't listen to what others define as success—most of their definitions will include things that will fade. Success is not so much a destination as it is a lifestyle. "Whatever you do, work at it with all your heart, as working for the Lord, not for men" (Colossians 3:23). Ask yourself if you are reaching toward a goal to achieve a destination or to live your life for Christ? Do you picture him as your audience or are you more concerned with pleasing others? Make a list of the things that are most important to you. Then ask yourself, "What is going to last?"

• **Stop spending time on things that aren't really important.** The Apostle Paul put it this way, "Be very careful, then, how you live—not as unwise but as wise, making the most of every opportunity, because the days are evil" (Ephesians 5:15-16). Paul was trying to stress the urgency of keeping our standards high and making wise decisions. Spending too much time in front of the TV may be fun, but it may also be a poor use of our time. When you're tempted to stay up late, watching a TV show, ask yourself, "Tomorrow morning when I get up, will I be glad that I stayed up an extra half-hour to play video games?"

Everything you do is influenced by what you think is important. Take some time this week to make sure you're not placing too much importance on things that will fade.

Legendary Joe ready to say it's so

The comeback Kid is going away again . . . for good. This time, it isn't back surgery sending him away. Or a bum elbow. Or a trade. It's a toast. Joe Montana—who has said with consistent sincerity, "When it's over, there's no coming back" —rides into the sunset with a grand, public retirement ceremony Tuesday in downtown San Francisco. Chapter closed. Script finished. Credits roll. So, this is what Montana, 38, meant by leaving on his terms. Two years to the week after his trade from the San Francisco 49ers to the Kansas City Chiefs left Bay Area fans emotionally torn, Big Sky is back to exit in style. Yo, Joe. Thanks for the memories. "Playing with him is like playing with Babe Ruth," 49ers tight end Brent Jones once reasoned. "He's the greatest. You can't help but appreciate that."

Joe's right, "When it's over, there's no coming back." Well . . . at least that's true for most athletes–unless you're Michael Jordan. For all athletes there comes a time that many think will never arrive. In fact, most are like Joe Montana whose first words on the day he announced his retirement were, "I thought I would never say the word "retirement."

Sports fans will eventually hear all of their favorite sports heroes admit that they've reached the end of their career without any hope of a return to the sport they love. Thankfully, for all of us who are committed to Christ, we know Jesus will make the ultimate comeback. There isn't any reason to believe that he won't make a final comeback. Before Jesus left earth to return to heaven, he promised, "I will come again" (John 14:30). There won't be any press conferences to announce his return. But we do know that our Savior will keep his promise. He clearly announced that he would one day make his return and it would come quickly (Revelation 22:12).

While the media anxiously awaited Montana's retirement announcement or Air Jordan's return, these events can't begin to compare to the excitement when Jesus returns to earth, "Look, he is coming with the clouds, and every eye will see him, even those who pierced him; and all the people of the earth will mourn because of him. So shall it be! Amen" (Revelation 1:7). It will be the largest media event in history. For those who have rejected him, it will be bitter disappointment and despair. But for those who have received him and await his return, it will bring joy and hope.

Do you look forward to His return? When Michael Jordan retired from basketball: the media, fans and Nike never lost site of a possible return—no matter how remote. The promise of Jesus' return isn't remote or a good possibility—it's definite. And this promise should give us hope and strength.

Are you prepared for Jesus' return? Here are a couple of thoughts on the greatest comeback the world will ever witness.

• **No Fear! Don't doubt for a moment that you are secure in God's love.** His promises are sound and His return is definite. No Fear!, shouldn't be just a slogan on sportswear. It needs to be our attitude toward life. Death is not fatal, nor is defeat final. It shouldn't matter if we face the greatest challenge of our lives on or off the playing field—there is nothing to fear with Christ as our Savior.

• **Plan for tomorrow, but live like Christ will return today.** Think about this: If you had the opportunity to meet Joe Montana or Michael Jordan tomorrow morning, how would you prepare? Would you clean your house, if they were coming to dinner? Would you think about what you might say and do? How about Jesus Christ? How would you live your life differently today, knowing Christ was going to return tomorrow? Would it influence the way you treat your friends and family? Don't take anything for granted. He never told us how soon He would return, but the fact that He will return should encourage us to live godly lives. Remember, Jesus Christ is the greatest! Take time to appreciate Him and His promise to return.

Police incident forces coach to leave position at Michigan

Gary Moeller says he still has his dignity, but what he does not have is his job. Following a drunken outburst last week that embarrassed his employer and startled his colleagues, Moeller resigned Thursday as football coach at Michigan. "This is one of the saddest days of my life," said Defensive coordinator Lloyd Carr who has been appointed interim coach. "A man I respect and have the utmost admiration for, is no longer here. I would not be honest If I say we are not wounded or felt great pain. I can't tell you what a terrible experience it was to see this proud man defeated. But he's tough. He will rebound."

Since I don't know Coach Moeller, I have no idea if this incident represents a pattern of his life or one night where he used extremely poor judgement. But I do know the Bible is clear when it comes to the value of our reputation. "A good name is more desirable than great riches; to be esteemed is better than silver or gold" (Proverbs 22:1).

Whether you are an athlete, coach or businessman, your reputation is much more valuable than you might think. Within just a few hours, Coach Moeller, managed to ruin his reputation and lose his job. He had served on the Michigan staff for 24 years and had led them to three Big Ten championships outright and tied for a fourth. He compiled a 44-13-3 overall record, including successive 8-4 seasons the past two seasons. Yet even his outstanding football record wasn't enough to save his job or more importantly his reputation.

Michigan's Athletic Director Joe Roberson said, "There is a higher standard for college coaches. Such standards are necessary for the integrity of a large institution like Michigan." To serve a human institution, like Michigan, brings with it certain responsibilities and standards. But what about service to God? Should our standards be less? And while each of us is probably not under the scrutiny of the public eye like a football coach, God does see all we do and say. Although our position in Christ is not in jeopardy when we blow it, thankfully we serve a forgiving God, our mistakes do grieve the God we serve.

Reputation is who people think you are, and character is actually who you are. What we think about Moeller is not nearly as important as his true character. We'll look at the importance of character later. Yet reputation does matter. God may be more concerned with character, but reputation is important to any football program, school or business. It doesn't take much to ruin a good reputation. A slip of the tongue or a temper that goes unchecked. What can we do to protect not only our reputation, but more importantly, God's reputation?

• **Don't put yourself in any situation that might compromise your reputation.** Joseph is an example of someone who made sure he removed himself from a compromising situation. "Now Joseph was handsome in form and appearance. And it came about after these events that his master's wife looked with desire at Joseph, and she said, 'Lie with me' . . . And he left his garment in her hand and fled, and went outside" (Genesis 39:1-12). He ran like mad and never looked back.

• **Join an accountability team.** Maybe it's a friend or your Bible study group. The Bible is clear in Eccles. 4:9, "Two are better than one because they have a good return for their work." *The Living Bible* puts it this way, "The results can be much better." There is a lot to gain by having someone hold us accountable to God's standards of conduct. They can help us gain and keep perspective. They can provide valuable objectivity. Sometimes just getting their input can make the difference between compromise or sticking to our principles.

Spurs prevail over Seattle on 'Character'

Even without Dennis Rodman, San Antonio won the battle of the boards against Seattle. With Rodman sidelined by a separated shoulder, Chuck Person and J.R. Reid filled the rebounding gap and helped the Spurs beat the visiting SuperSonics 104-96 Monday night. Person and Reid each grabbed 11 rebounds, helping San Antonio outrebound Seattle 53-45. "That was a character win," Spurs Coach Bob Hill said. "After the news about Dennis, I can't say enough about these guys. They were on a mission. Tonight's performance was real special."

Character counts, no doubt about it. Ask any coach or NBA owner if character is important and you'll quickly find out that it really does count. But what is character? Is it only the ability to perform when the odds are against you? Or is it much more? Here are some thoughts about character:

"The highest reward for a man's toil, is not what he gets for it, but rather what he becomes by it."
–American Way

"God is more concerned about our character than our comfort. His goal is not to pamper us physically but to perfect us spiritually."
–Paul W. Powell

"Only what we have wrought into our character during life can we take with us."
–Humboldt

"Sow a thought, reap an act; sow an act, reap a habit; sow a habit, reap a character; sow a character, reap a destiny."

"Character, is what we do when no one else is looking."

Character is a word that is used only a few times in the Bible. It's a word that is rarely used or shown on prime time TV. Yet we recognize it when we see it. Most people define character by the lack of it. They look around at the moral collapse in our society and point to examples of cheating, lying and drug abuse and know that we lack character. Many feel like they're sinking in the quicksand of immoral behavior.

Character is the person God sees when He looks at us. And it's not always the same person that our closest friends see, "God sees not as man sees, for man looks at the outward appearance, but the Lord looks at the heart" (1 Samuel 16:7).

Now let's face it—when God looks at our hearts, He won't see perfection. Hopefully, what He will see is growth toward Christlikeness. In fact, our greatest concern in life should be character growth. It involves a change of lifestyle. It means an adjustment in our attitudes and actions. In short, spiritual growth and character development occur when God's Word makes a practical and positive change in the way we live our lives.

• **Be a doer of God's Word.** Don't rely on church attendance, being busy for God, or education for spiritual growth. It's not only knowing the right stuff, but rather doing the right things that produces character. "Do not merely listen to the word, and so deceive yourselves. Do what it says" (James 1:22).

• **Live a Christlike life so that others might be inspired to do what is right.** We need men and women who are ready to lead by example (Matthew 5:16).

Robinson drives Spurs; Rodman rides bench

While Dennis Rodman sat and watched, David Robinson took the Los Angeles Lakers apart. Robinson scored 26 points, grabbed 22 rebounds and played his usual excellent defense while leading the Spurs past the Lakers 80-71 for a lead in the NBA Western Conference Semifinal. Rodman angered Spurs Coach Bob Hill when he failed to participate in a huddle during the second half in game 3. After being replaced, he took his shoes off, wrapped a towel around his head and proceeded to lie down on the court.

What words come to mind when you think of Dennis Rodman? Unpredictable? Strange? Disruptive? Intensity? Eccentric? Disrespectful? All of these words may describe the man fans have come to call the "worm." I've got one more word for the type of behavior he demonstrated in the semifinal game–self-centered. Many athletes struggle with self-centeredness since recognition is at the heart of competition. San Antonio Coach Bob Hill put it this way, "I think a lot of these kids today are the products of no discipline in schools. When we were in school, if we did something wrong, we'd be disciplined. Today, none of that happens. Now you've got these young guys who went to school with no discipline. Then they get recruited to play basketball in college, and they get paid. Then they come out of school early and expect to make millions of dollars in the NBA."

Whether it's a lack of discipline at school or home, ego and self-centeredness are at the heart of the problem. But these problems are not exclusive to athletes. In fact, even Jesus' disciples struggled with their own selfish ambitions of being the greatest in God's kingdom. When the disciples argued over who should be number one, Jesus taught his men an important truth about ego, "They came to Capernaum. When he was in the house, he asked them, 'What were you arguing about on the road?' But they kept quiet because on the way they had argued about who was the greatest. Sitting down, Jesus called the Twelve and said, 'If anyone wants to be first, he must be the very last, and the servant of all'" (Mark 9:33-35).

In sports, greatness is often defined as status. The number of games won. An MVP award. A championship trophy. Or the size of your contract. But God determines greatness in His kingdom by service, not status. Jesus' disciples failed to grasp God's view of greatness. The phrase, "he must be the very last," describes putting another person's interests ahead of your own. So if you want to be great in God's eyes, put the emphasis on others, rather than drawing attention to yourself.

• **Compare your motives with christ's.** It's not easy to compare our motives to Christ's. That's why the disciples were afraid to answer Jesus' questions. They were wrapped up in their own personal success and were embarrassed to answer His question. It's not wrong to be ambitious, but when ambition becomes more important than obedience, it becomes sin. Pride can often cause us to overvalue our position or rewards from sports or other areas of life. Compare your motives with Christ's and choose His way, not the world's.

• **Become great by putting other people ahead of your own interest.** If you really want to be great, then try to do your best to serve others. Following Rodman's benching, his replacement, Terry Cummings, said, "You can never allow one player to be more important than the team." The smart teams, the teams that collect championships like trading cards, are the ones who understand that you must not serve only self. And on God's team, it not only serves the best interest of the team–but God commands us to be great by serving others.

Bagwell stuck in big slump

Perhaps no major leaguer is having a more disappointing season than Jeff Bagwell, last year's NL MVP. Bagwell was hitting .173 heading into the weekend with two homers and nine RBIs. He has struck out 27 times in 75 at-bats and has just seven singles. "Everybody goes through periods like these. I don't care how good you are or what you did last year, every career is going to have a slump at one point or another. I've taken some extra BP, but I do that periodically anyway. The only way this ends is Jeff Bagwell working out of it and that is what I am working on."

Bagwell is right about slumps–we all go through them. Michael Jordan, Steve Young and Jeff Bagwell share one thing in common– slumps! And we do, too. Fortunately for Bagwell, he understands that you don't blame others for your slump, but you find a way to work out of it. Have you heard anyone this week blame someone else for their own problems? A couple of years ago, the Dallas Cowboys place kicker was asked why he missed a field goal in a game against the Houston Oilers. "I was too busy reading my stats on the scoreboard." He later missed another one, he said the stadium's grass was "too tall." Yet in another game he said, "My helmet was too tight and it was squeezing my brain." Once he even blamed the holder for placing the ball upside down.

While you and I might laugh at this example, we've all made excuses for poor performance or a bad attitude. How does a Christian work through a slump? Let's begin by recognizing that your thoughts control your actions. If you want to change the way you hit, you must first change how you think. Psychology discovered this truth in the last century, but Solomon taught this principle thousands of years earlier. "Be careful how you think; your life is shaped by your thoughts" (Proverbs 4:23 Good News). Here are four guidelines for changing the way you think about any slump.

• **Put your trust in God.** According to Proverbs 3:5-6 and other passages, you should put your trust in God and depend on Him. You can chose to rely on yourself, but doesn't it make more sense to place your faith in the One who created you? Just as a head coach is the best person to direct his team, in a similar way, God is in the best position to guide you through your slumps.

• **Pray and believe God is sufficient.** In the words of the Apostle Paul in Philippians 4:6-7, we are to pray about all of our circumstances, "Do not be anxious about anything, but in everything, by prayer and petition, with thanksgiving, present your requests to God. And the peace of God, which transcends all understanding, will guard your hearts and minds in Christ Jesus." Whatever your request is, do you regularly and diligently, bring it to God in prayer, trusting that He will help you? If not, why not? God is able. The Bible says it over and over. "Do you not know? Have you not heard? The Lord is the everlasting God, the Creator of the ends of the earth. He will not grow tired or weary" (Isaiah 40:28). He is able to control nature, alter circumstances and change people.

• **Choose to be joyful.** Happiness depends on circumstances, but joy can happen in spite of a slump. Outlook determines outcome, and attitude determines action. A joyful attitude is essential when working through a slump. James says, "Consider it pure joy, my brothers, whenever you face trials of many kinds" (James 1:2).

• **Forget the past, focus on the goal.** You must learn from the past, but do not be controlled by it. Any runner who looks backward while running forward risks losing the race. The Apostle Paul gives several ways to apply this truth. "Brothers, I do not consider myself yet to have taken hold of it . But one thing I do: Forgetting what is behind and straining toward what is ahead, I press on toward the goal to win the prize for which God has called me heavenward in Christ Jesus" (Philippians 3:13-14).

After 5 years, founder's message cuts to the heart

As the Promise Keepers band soared into the anthem "Godly Men," Bill McCartney stood and lifted his hands high in praise to God. "Lord help us turn from sin and begin again, as godly men," sang the former University of Colorado football coach, along with 52,000 men who last weekend filled RFK Stadium in Washington, D.C. McCartney took to the pulpit to urge the crowd to repent, be faithful to their wives, serve their families, support their brothers and stop worshiping their careers. But this sermon had a twist. Five years after his first vision of men packing stadiums, McCartney explained how this message finally cut into his heart and left him in the position of needing to heed his own altar call. "For 32 years my wife had chased Bill McCartney's dreams, not Lyndi's dreams. She was married to a man who was so focused, so driven, so possessed . . . It was like God opened my eyes." The coach concluded by saying that he had been sinfully selfish—a taker, not a giver. As the 1994 regular season ended, he took advantage of an exit clause in his 15-year contract.

Practice what you preach. It's sounds so simple–yet many of us find it difficult to do. Most of us can relate to McCartney. Who hasn't blown it at one time or another? But it's also an issue of putting first things first, isn't it? Whether you're a football coach or a student, it's not easy to stop and think and then do things in the order of their importance. We all have more things to do than we have time. So it's important to sort out how to properly think through our priorities. Here are some questions to think through:

- How involved should I be in the church? In other organizations? In athletics?
- How can I cultivate a close relationship with family members?
- How should I try to reach co-workers and friends for Christ?
- What are my goals for family and career?

Make your own list of questions this week. It will take time, but anything worth doing is worth taking the time to do right. Here are some guidelines for putting first things first.

• **Ask God for direction by praying and being quiet.** The report on McCartney later said, "History is full of fierce, focused and even fanatical religious leaders who light spiritual fires and then fall in flames–often taking their movements with them. McCartney is trying to back away from the abyss, settling into a life of private prayer and public speaking. The general will try to go on retreat. 'Everyone in (Promise Keepers) is so busy. The numbers are expanding so rapidly. Everyone is caught up in a beehive of activity. Somebody has to stop and be quiet before the Lord,' McCartney said." Jesus knew how important it was to be quiet. Mark 6:31 says, "Then, because so many people were coming and going that they did not even have a chance to eat, he (Jesus) said to them, 'Come with me by yourselves to a quiet place and get some rest.'"

• **Decide on a game plan.** Back off and think through your plans. Make a game plan for every area of your life. Jesus said, "For which one of you, when he wants to build a tower, does not first sit down and calculate the cost, to see if he has enough to complete it" (Luke 14:28).

• **Don't just be a list-maker–be a list-keeper.** McCartney's wife, Lyndi, in her husband's newly revised autobiography, describes his struggle with keeping his commitments. "I told him I needed to be on his calendar, so he began penciling me in. But then I got erased a couple of times. So I went back and told him I wanted to be written in ink–'it's ink or nothing,' I said." It's ironic that even the founder of a movement based on being a promise keeper, struggled with keeping his own promises. As difficult as it is, God commands us to keep our commitments (James 1:22).

Tension at the ballpark

Sure, it's hot and humid, but maybe something else has cranked up baseball temperatures and contributed to recent player-fan flare-ups. "We're a lot like a couple that's fighting and trying to get back together", says Eric Yaverbaum, founder of a New York-based fan group called Strike Back. "We want the relationship to work, but you know there's tension when a guy walks off the field and gives Yankee Stadium the finger." Yankees pitcher Jack McDowell made the gesture after being booed at home. Meanwhile, the American League is looking into an altercation between California Angels outfielder Chili Davis and a fan in Milwaukee, and Baltimore reliever Doug Jones doffed his cap when Orioles fans booed him after he blew a four-run lead in the ninth. Yaverbaum predicts an eventual reconciliation. "Fans want to be in love with the players again. Players want to have the same relationship they had with the fans. But that's not happening this season."

I've discovered three types of athletes and fans: Accusers, excusers and choosers. There's no doubt that the 1994 baseball strike has created plenty of accusers and excusers during the past year. Whether it's players looking for excuses for poor performance or fans that accuse them of giving less than their best, baseball needs reconciliation between fans and players.

There is even a greater need for reconciliation among different races in our society. When talking about racial reconciliation, I've found that most of us fit into one of these categories.

Accusers will blame others for everything. Applied to race reconciliation, some white people tend to blame their problems on Affirmative Action programs and say things like, "Blacks act like we (whites) owe them some special favors because of something we had nothing to do with." On the other side, some blacks accuse whites of refusing to give them opportunities because of the color of their skin. "That guy didn't even consider me for the promotion because I'm black!"

While excusers don't always play the blame game, they do have an excuse for everything. George Washington Carver said, "Ninety nine percent of all failures come from people who've perfected the habit of making excuses." When it comes to race issues it's easy to blame others for our circumstances (economics) or background (environment). But each time we make excuses for our behavior we move further away from the solution. When whites are asked why they don't do something about racism in the 90's, some will say, "I don't know any blacks and besides a lot of them are doing okay today." When blacks are asked the same question, some will say, "They (whites) don't have any idea what we've been through–they just don't understand us."

The Apostle Paul realized that neither the accuser or excuser view is biblical. He and his co-worker, Barnabas, had worked hard to bring together two groups of people in Antioch, Jews and Gentiles. Antioch was the first true multiracial church. This early church became the base of operation for Paul and Barnabas.

This multiracial team of believers made an impact on others because it refused to accuse or excuse racial separation. The choices they faced are no different than the choices we have today. We can choose to disagree with one another and split along racial lines. But the result will be two different churches. It's been said that the most segregated time in America, during the week, is Sunday morning at church. Even though we may agree to disagree, rather than confront our differences, we will still remain two separate groups.

God's choice for us is unity built through communication and conflict. It may be a fight, but it's a battle that's worth fighting. Paul fought for unity in 1 Corinthians 1:10: "I appeal to you, brothers in the name of our Lord Jesus Christ, that all of you agree with one another so that there may be no divisions among you and that you may be perfectly united in mind and thought."

All of us need to confess racial prejudice. Our responsibility is to choose to be a reconciler, like the Apostle Paul. The early church struggled with reconciliation, but eventually they became one body–Jew, Greek, Samaritan and Gentile–proving that God can bring any race together. Choose to be the type of person that God can use to bring unity to the body of Christ. After all, someday we will spend eternity together. Isn't it about time you met your future teammates?

Teammates' remember Mantle

Mickey Mantle's team filled the Lovers Lane United Methodist Church where Mantle had not been a member, a church that was large enough and glorious enough to suit the funeral of a sporting hero and national icon. One member of this team had been with Mantle through the last days. Mantle may have jokingly called Bobby Richardson a "milk drinker" in their Yankee days, but Mantle had never flaunted his escapades or his language around the born-again Christian in a nearby locker. The former second baseman, now a lay preacher, recalled in the sermon how he had witnessed his faith to Mantle a few times when they were with the Yankees, only to detect "a fear of death, an emptiness he tried to cover with harmful choices." When Mantle knew his cancer had returned in July, he made a call to Richardson and asked him to pray, over the telephone. And last week Richardson was asked to come to Dallas. Mickey said, "Bobby, I want you to know I've accepted Christ as my Savior," Richardson said Tuesday. And Richardson discovered Mantle had been listening to him, many years earlier.

Mickey Mantle was without a doubt the hero of at least two generations of baseball fans. I'm sure I was one of his biggest fans. I collected more than a hundred Mantle baseball cards. I played with a genuine Folger's Coffee Mickey Mantle glove. I used to swing, run and even limp like he did (comedian Billy Crystal wasn't the only Yankee fan who imitated Mantle). He seemed to represent all that was good in sports. He played hard, hit the booming home runs, and never let injuries keep him from making the clutch play. In fact, *Sports Illustrated* put it this way, "Mickey Mantle was the last great player on the last great team."

Like any sport legend, there are valuable lessons we can all learn from his life. Here are a couple from Mickey Mantle's life.

• **Failure is never final.** Mantle proved that failure is never final. Throughout his career he was able to comeback from all kinds of injuries and adversity. Yet in life, his drinking and off-field escapades turned deadly. Forty years of hard drinking left him in a battle against liver cancer that he couldn't win. He had abused his body and he would eventually suffer the consequences. But during the final year of his life he admitted his alcoholism and got treatment for his problem. Bob Costas summed-up Mantle's final days during the eulogy. "And then in the end, something remarkable happened–the way it does for champions. Mickey Mantle rallied. His heart took over, and he had some innings as fine as any in 1956 or with his buddy, Roger in 1961. But this time, he did it in the harsh and trying summer of '95. And what he did was stunning. The sheer grace of the ninth inning–the humility, the sense of humor, the total absence of self pity, the simple eloquence and honesty of his pleas to others to take heed of his mistakes." The Bible puts it this way, "The one who confesses and forsakes his mistakes get another chance" (Proverbs 28:13).

All of us at one time or another have taken the ball and run in the wrong direction. We all have stumbled and and fumbled our way through life, but God says, "Get up and get back in the game. It isn't over yet!"

• **Never, never, never . . . stop praying and sharing your faith with others.** It took Mickey Mantle his entire life to discover what Solomon discovered years before. "I said to myself, 'Come now, I will test you with pleasure. So enjoy yourself.' And behold, it too was futility" (Ecclesiastes 2:1). Solomon's statement could be paraphrased, "I found no lasting values in this attempt." Toward the end of his life, Mantle realized the empty pursuit of self and found lasting value in a relationship with Jesus Christ. Thankfully, he had a teammate, like Bobby Richardson, who never quit praying and sharing his faith with Mickey.

When Bobby Richardson spoke at Mantle's funeral he shared the poem, "God's Hall of Fame." A part of the poem reads, "The Hall of fame is only good as long as time shall be; But keep in mind, God's Hall of Fame is for eternity; to have your name inscribed up there is greater more by far than all the fame and all the praise of every man-made star." In the end, he faced death with the knowledge that he had joined God's Hall of Fame. Mick was only partially right when he said, "I'm not a role model. Don't be like me." In the ninth inning of his life he became what we all thought he was in the '50s and '60s–a true role model.

Kicker takes stand against Playboy

In 1994, University of Texas freshman kicker Phil Dawson had a super year with the football team. And as a result, he was named to Playboy Magazine's 39th Annual Preseason All-American team. As a Christian, that's something that didn't suit him. And he told the magazine so. "Basically, all I heard was that no matter what I decided to do, I was still selected to that team." But Playboy finally relented and selected someone else. Dawson said he had no interest in being connected with the king of soft pornography, in spite of the enticement of an all-expense paid weekend at the Playboy Mansion in Phoenix. Dawson says many of his teammates don't understand his decision. And when they ask, he uses it as an opportunity to share his faith.

We live in a time when society's values have been turned upside down. Just 30 years ago, things we listen to, read, or watch would have been considered wrong. Some scholars argue that we have lowered our standards and that we are now living in a post-Christian era. In fact, many believe that humanism has reached an all-time high. False solutions are offered in every area of life.

Athough these times may be difficult, the Apostle Paul offers us some advice on how to handle times like these, "Preach the Word; be prepared in season and out of season; correct, rebuke and encourage—with great patience and careful instruction. For the time will come when men will not put up with sound doctrine. Instead, to suit their own desires, they will gather around them a great number of teachers to say what their itching ears want to hear. They will turn their ears away from the truth and turn aside to myths. But you, keep your head in all situations, endure hardship, do the work of an evangelist, discharge all the duties of your ministry" (2 Timothy 4: 2-5).

Phil Dawson demonstrated that it is still possible to walk with God and take a stand against popular culture. Based upon Paul's advice, here is how we can be faithful in times like these:

• **Make the Bible your playbook for life.** Many segments of our society have a tendency to push aside Scripture and substitute the wisdom of men and women. Whether it's to prevent drug use or teen pregnancy, many so-called experts offer their best advice which falls far short of God's advice, if it neglects the Bible. Any program, even with the best intentions, makes a terrible mistake by overlooking God's blueprint for life. Phil Dawson made his decision to refuse Playboy's offer because he was following God's directives for his life. Dawson, later said in an interview with *Sharing The Victory,* "Many people respected my position, but some didn't understand. Taking Playboy's offer was not right for me with what I'm trying to do with my life."

• **Be ready to respond.** Every athlete understands the need for preparation. Without preparation, we can be more easily influenced by wrong-headed thinking. Paul's advice to be ready means to "be at hand, to have an alert mind." It's the idea of being ready to serve God in any situation, whether or not it is convenient. Think biblically about the important issues of our day and be sensitive to how God may want you to respond.

• **Take a stand.** Sooner or later, each of us is responsible for our actions. At some point during a game, an athlete must step forward and make the shot or pass that will help determine the outcome of the game. For the Christian, taking a stand means correcting, rebuking and encouraging–when it's appropriate. It means doing the right thing, even when others around us don't.

Phil Dawson kicks off the season by taking a stand against soft pornography. His decision is based upon God's Word and he is ready to not only take a stand against impurity, but to also use the situation as an opportunity to share his faith with others. Can we do anything less in our lives?

'Field of Dreams' is drawing more people than ever to Northeast Iowa's 'Heaven'

"Field of Dreams" is a movie about redemption and reconciliation, about an Iowa farmer named Ray Kinsella who heard voices in his cornfield and heeded them. "If you build it, he will come," the first voice said. Ray Kinsella wound up with a ballfield where his corn used to be, with Shoeless Joe Jackson and the other 1919 Black Sox walking out from the stalks to play there; and finally, with his own father as a young man standing before him, the two of them playing a game of catch together, spectral father and real-life son, connected in a way they never had been. Unlike many small farming communities, the local economy of Dyersville (pop. 3,800), is flourishing from the field that was built for this hit movie starring Kevin Costner. An estimated 55,000 people will visit this year, more than ever before.

Why do people visit? No doubt some simply want to see the site of a famous movie location. Others may be seeking the redemption and reconciliation that is the theme of "Field of Dreams." In fact, the executive director of the Dyersville Chamber of Commerce, tells the story of two brothers who hadn't spoken to each other for 30 years. They met on the field by chance, and settled their differences with one another. It's clear that visitors to the field believe it is much more than grass and dirt. ESPN even did a documentary about the people who make pilgrimages to the field. It was called "Dreamsfield."

Redemption and reconciliation are themes that tug at our hearts. Not many of us can sit through the final minutes of "Field of Dreams," when Costner reconciles with his father by symbolically playing catch, without shedding a few tears. The movie is about much more than baseball. Its theme of redemption and reconciliation make it a story that is more about spirituality than baseball.

For the Christian, the movie is a rerun of another familiar story about redemption and reconciliation—the parable of the lost son. If there had been a movie preview for this story, it would have shown a younger son taking his inheritance and eventually blowing it on wild living. But just like "Field of Dreams" the parable of the lost son ends with the son seeking redemption and reconciliation. With both stories there are important lessons about life none of us should forget.

• **Some people need to hit bottom before they come to their senses.** The younger son, like many in our society had to hit bottom before he came to his senses. "He longed to fill his stomach with the pods that the pigs were eating, but no one gave him anything. When he came to his senses, he said, 'How many of my father's hired men have food to spare, and here I am starving to death'" (Luke 15:16-17). His statement shows how far he had sunk in his life. According to Moses' law, pigs were considered unclean and were not to be eaten or used for sacrifices. For any Jew to be reduced to feeding pigs would have been a tremendous humiliation. Unfortunately, for some people it takes years before they hit bottom and come to their senses. For former Yankee Mickey Mantle, it wasn't until the end of his life, when his drinking had gotten so bad that he could barely remember one day from the next.

• **God waits patiently for us to come to our senses—we should do likewise for others, too.** God's love is patient. He waits for us to respond to His love and acceptance. He doesn't treat us like robots. He gives us the opportunity to respond to Him, but He never forces us to to come to Him. Like the father of the lost son, God waits patiently for us to come to our senses.

• **Be willing to forgive and accept someone who offends you, rather than get revenge.** The older brother couldn't forgive and forget the injustice he felt his brother had caused his family. The older brother's anger and bitterness left him just as lost as his brother. In "Field of Dreams," Ray Kinsella's life was not complete until he was finally able to forgive his father. So, too, our lives can never be complete without God's patient love and forgiveness.

Psychology major tries training above the shoulders

Mike Marsh is engaged in some mind-body experimentation this summer. Too bad the sprinter can't get credit toward the graduate courses in educational psychology he takes at the University of Houston. "I'm interested in psychology and the biological effect on the mind and vice versa. It has so much to do with what I'm doing now. I believe that psychological factors are the greater portion of what determines if an athlete is mediocre as opposed to great. At the world-class level, the variation in talent level is minuscule. But there's going to be a visible spread between first and eighth. That's mental," says Marsh.

Marsh's fast thinking probably had a lot to do with his win at the U.S. 100-meter Championships that June. The principles that Marsh believes any runner should follow are: 1) Stay relaxed in a tense situation. 2) Not dwell on the result if they want to win. "The principles behind running fast never change. My responsibility is to always run well, whether first or eighth," says Marsh.

Not bad advice. In fact, the same approach can easily be applied to life. But Marsh wasn't the first person to train above his shoulders. The Apostle Paul did a bit of fast thinking himself.

• **Stay relaxed in a tense situation.** One of the principles God teaches us through the Apostle Paul is the concept of isolation. In this concept, you isolate the past from your mind and totally concentrate on your goal. Paul was completely focused on his ultimate goal—to become conformed to the likeness of Jesus. He wrote: "Brothers, I do not consider myself yet to have taken hold of it. But one thing I do: Forgetting what is behind and straining toward what is ahead, I press on toward the goal to win the prize for which God has called me heavenward in Christ Jesus" (Philippians 3:13-14). Paul teaches us two ways to stay relaxed in any situation.

First, forget the past. The word Paul uses for "forgetting" in Philippians 3:13-14, means he totally forgot. The event was no longer in his conscious mind. It's the idea of putting the event behind you. If we fail to isolate the past from the present, we run the risk of tensing-up during competition. After all, who hasn't felt somewhat nervous following failure in the athletic arena? For example: If you have been soundly beaten by your opponent in tennis, then the natural reaction would be nervousness when you face him/her in the next match. Don't dwell on the past

Second, Paul teaches us to pursue our goal. The word "press" actually means to pursue–to actively go after something. It's focusing all of your energy on achieving your goal. Paul's point is: By no longer thinking about the past, you can't completely leave the event behind. But by putting the event in the past, and then, by deliberately focusing your attention on the goal, you can stay relaxed. The positive action of focusing on the goal keeps the negative experience from influencing you.

Be sure to practice isolation following every event, whether it's good or bad. The attitude of disappointment or over-confidence, will not be a problem if you purse the ultimate goal of Christ-likeness.

• **Not dwell on the result if they want to win.** The best way to not dwell on the result is to focus on the process or journey, rather than the result. The Bible defines winning by the effort toward our goal of Christ-likeness, rather than the result on the scoreboard. "Whatever you do, work at it with all your heart, as working for the Lord, not for men" (Colossians 3:23). If we leave the scoreboard results to God, then we won't waste our time and energy on worrying about the outcome.

Marsh's fast thinking is correct. "My responsibility is to always run well, whether first or eighth." If we focus on our responsibilities, rather than the results, than we can maximize our God-given talents and abilities.

Orioles' Iron Man Eclipses Gehrig Mark

Cal Ripkin, whose boyhood dream was to be good enough to play in the minor leagues like his dad, played in his 2,131 consecutive major league game Wednesday night, replacing the immortal Lou Gehrig as guard of one of baseball's most revered accomplishments. Gehrig, the Iron Horse of the New York Yankees, held the record since April 30, 1939.

Persistence. The word is the perfect description of Cal Ripkin. What Cal Ripkin did seems to define the word, "persistence." He broke the unbreakable record. Most experts and fans thought Lou Gehrig's record consecutive game mark would never fall. A 20-year-old rookie with the Boston Red Sox, Ted Williams, watched Lou Gehrig deliver his "luckiest man on the face of the Earth" speech in 1939. Williams, 77, was just as amazed to watch Cal Ripkin tie the "insurmountable record." Williams said, "I kept thinking about how great a player Lou was and about the 2,130 consecutive games. I was just a kid and it was hard to believe. That was a record I never thought would be broken. I don't think I ever played in more than 26 in a row. Some players today get shampoo in their eyes and land on the disabled list."

Here are several thoughts on persistence and determination.

"Nothing in the world can take the place of persistence. Talent will not. Nothing is more common than unsuccessful men with talent. Genius will not; unrewarded genius is almost a proverb. Education will not; the world is full of educated derelicts. Persistence and determination alone are omnipotent." Calvin Coolidge

"Many people fail in life because they believe in the adage: If you don't succeed, try something else. But success eludes those who follow such advice. Virtually everyone has had dreams at one time or another, especially in youth. the dreams that have come true did so because people stuck to their ambitions. They refused to be discouraged. They never let disappointment get the upper hand. Challenges only spurred them on to greater effort." Don Owens

"When Jesus tells us to "seek first the kingdom of God," the very word "seek" implies a strong-minded pursuit. *J.B. Phillips* paraphrases the idea with "set your heart on." *The Amplified Bible* says, "Aim at and strive after." The Greek text of Matthew's Gospel states a continual command: "Keep on continually seeking . . ." The thought is determination, which I define as "deciding to hang tough, regardless." Charles Swindoll

Persistence and determination are two important character qualities needed by every Christian. You see, the spiritual life of a Christian is much more like a cross-country run than a sprint. And those who don't fizzle out at the end of the race are people who don't get discouraged. If you want to know someone's character, examine how they respond to adversity. Criticism and failure often revel more about a person's character than success. How do you respond when things don't go your way? Someone unjustly criticizes you? When you fall short of your expectations? When everything seems to go against you?

As a Christian, you don't need to gut it out on your own. It's a matter of relying on God for your strength. God can do amazing things through us, by His power. Jesus said, "... apart from me you can do nothing" (John 15:5). The Apostle Paul said, "Now to him who is able to do immeasurably more than all we ask or imagine, according to his power that is at work within us" (Ephesians 3:20).

Remember, when you are faced with an impossible situation, stretch out your courage, hang tough and depend on Him. The Bible says, "Let us not get tired of doing what is right, for after a while we will reap at harvest of blessing, if we don't get discouraged and give up" (Galatians 6:9). Allow God to make you into His "Iron Man." He alone provides the power and the strength to enable us to consecutively serve Him each day of our lives. "I can do all things through Christ who gives me the strength" (Philippians 4:13).

Fryar blows kisses to crowd

Irving Fryar, the former New England wide receiver who Sunday returned to his former stomping grounds in a Miami Dolphins uniform, was told some Patriots fans wished he never left. Before responding to that statement, Fryar gave a look that spoke a thousand words—beginning with, "Oh really? There are a lot of Patriots fans who felt I left too late, that I should have left quicker," said Fryar, who continued his dominance against his old team Sunday. Yet Fryar's sentiments about Patriots fans undoubtedly stemmed in part from the negative reaction he received after his 31-yard touchdown pass in the second quarter that gave the Dolphins a 17-3 lead. In response, Fryar, now an ordained minister, blew kisses at the crowd. "The Bible says love your enemies, and they were acting like they were my enemies," said Fryar. "They were booing me and spitting on me and calling me all kinds of names—everything but a child of God. They did that to Jesus, and I try to emulate Jesus and Jesus loved his enemies. That's all I can do, pray for them and tell them I love them and hopefully Jesus will touch them, too."

While Fryar's dominance on the field against his former teammates is impressive, it's not nearly as impressive as his reaction to the name-calling Patriot fans. Not even an outstanding athletic performance can equal the act of showing love toward those who hate you. And nowhere is the meaning of true love taught more clearly than in Scripture.

"But I tell you: Love your enemies and pray for those who persecute you, that you may be sons of your Father in heaven. He causes His sun to rise on the evil and the good, and sends rain on the righteous and the unrighteous. If you love those who love you, what reward will you get? Are not even the tax collectors doing that? And if you greet only your brothers, what are you doing more than others? Do not even pagans do that? Be perfect, therefore, as your heavenly Father is perfect" (Matthew 5:44-48).

Jesus' directed his remarks toward a group of religious teachers known as the Scribes and Pharisees who were proud, prejudiced, judgmental and vengeful men who acted with a holier-than-thou attitude. For this group of men, Jesus' teaching must have seemed crazy. After all, these so-called spiritual leaders not only felt they had the right to hate their enemies but the duty to hate their enemies.

Jesus' exposed this perverted teaching by commanding the religious teachers to love their enemies. The concept of loving your personal enemy wasn't even new—the Old Testament taught it, but the religious teachers had ignored God's truth. The problem the religious teachers had with Jesus' teaching is not much different than our problem today with loving our enemies. All of us tend to base love on the desirability of the object of our love. We love attractive people, recreation that is fun, hobbies that we enjoy, and things we own that impress others and look good. But God's love is need-oriented. When the Good Samaritan sacrificed his own convenience, resources and safety to meet another's needs, he demonstrated true love.

The Bible uses four different terms for the word "love." The love Jesus is talking about here is Agape, the love that seeks and works to meet another's highest good. This type of love might involve emotion, but it always involves action. A great example of this is Paul's teaching on love in 1 Corinthians 13, where all 15 character-istics of love are given in verb form.

Don't retaliate when someone attacks you. Instead, by loving and praying for our enemies we can overcome evil with good. No one demonstrated this more than Jesus himself. Can you imagine the pain of betrayal Jesus must have felt when he was unjustly put to death on the cross? Most of us will never know the anxiety and stress that Jesus experienced the last days of his life. But his example of overcoming evil with love should inspire us to do likewise. After all, each one of us were his enemy until we became one of his followers.

Irving Fryar is right. All we can do is "pray for them and tell them we love them and hopefully Jesus will touch them, too." You may not blow kisses at your enemies, but you can begin to take action to love them.

Giants' Bonds 'Under Stress' Part 1

As the San Francisco Giants slide closer to elimination from the playoff race, Barry Bonds says he is under so much stress and so tired of being blamed for everything that he may consider retiring. Bonds, 31, says he wakes up every morning with a migraine headache. He spends many nights getting booed by fans, both at home and on the road, who see him as the epitome of everything wrong with baseball. "It's everything, man. Look at my year. A lot of things, not just the game itself," he said Friday night. "I'm tired of taking blame for everyone else's problems. I don't need it. I'm going to sit down with my parents and grandparents after the season and talk to them and maybe talk to (Giants) owners and see where I'll go from there," Bonds said.

An old Greek motto says:

You will break the bow if you keep it always bent.

Stress is caused by two opposing forces which pull against each other. Whether it's the force of a bow being bent or the pressure of unhappy fans, stress adds undue pressure to our lives. Sometimes stress is created by the demands others place on us. Their "shoulds" and "musts" hit us like a linebacker sacking a quarterback.

Stress can be overcome by using God's strategy to defeat worry. And here are the signals from God's Word. Notice that I've marked where it's your responsibility to tackle worry and where it's God's responsibility to tackle worry.

Trust (my part) in the Lord with all your heart, and do not lean (my part) on your own understanding. In all your ways acknowledge (my part) Him, and He will make your paths straight (God's part) (Proverbs 3:5-6).

It's important to understand several of these key terms in Proverbs. Here is a breakdown of their meaning using football as an illustration.

• **Trust.** When a receiver runs a pass route, the quarterback places his trust in his receiver to run the correct play. If his receiver turns the wrong way or stops short on his pass pattern, the quarterback's throw is off the mark. The idea of trust in this verse is throwing oneself down and lying extended on the ground, casting all hopes for the present and the future on another. We are to place our complete trust in the Lord with all of our heart. How many times have you heard someone refer to a player who competes with a lot of heart? When John Madden refers to a football player with heart, he doesn't mean the organ in the chest that pumps blood. He's talking about the same thing the Bible refers to as one's "inner person" . . . that part of us which represents our emotion, intellect and will. It's the idea of not holding anything back.

• **Do not lean.** This is a negative command—maybe the best comparison is an defensive lineman who is warned not to lean into the neutral zone. Otherwise, he is likely to be flagged for being offsides. The idea in this verse is don't lean on your own ingenuity to work out your problems. In college football it's oftentimes the freshman who make mental mistakes. In the NFL it's rookies that for their lack of understanding blow it. It's often because they try to work things out on their own, rather than asking for advice or spending time in their playbook. In this verse in Proverbs it's a warning about relying too much on human understanding, rather than God's wisdom.

Next we'll look at the last two terms and how you can manage your stress. Remember to completely trust in God and don't place your understanding of a stressful situation on yourself.

Saints fans in disfavor with Coach (Stress Part 2)

Four years ago, when the New Orleans Saints were breaking San Francisco's stranglehold on the NFC West, the signs read, "Jim Mora for Governor." These days the Saints are 0-5 and fans are wearing paper bags and waving "Fire Mora" banners. On Sunday, 43,938 fans, the smallest Superdome crowd for a non-strike game since 1986, chanted "Mora must go!" as the clock ticked down. Forgotten is Mora's string of success—first coach to guide the Saints to a winning season; first to capture a division title; most victories ever by a Saints' coach; first to get the team to the playoffs. Under obvious pressure since training camp, Mora raged at reporters after a number of players were accused of rape in the dorm, charges the prosecutor refused to pursue.

Charles H. Mayo had this to say about worry and stress:

Worry affects circulation, the heart, the glands, the whole nervous system. I have never known a man who died from overwork, but many who died from doubt.

Sports has plenty of stressful moments. When competition requires two sides to push and pull against each other–there will be some stress. Although coaches probably feel the greatest amount of stress, no athlete is immune from it. In 1961, Yankee slugger Roger Maris actually lost clumps of his hair from the stress he felt on his way to breaking Babe Ruth's single-season home run record.

Let's continue our look at God's remedy for stress found in Proverbs with the final two parts.

Trust (my part) in the Lord with all your heart, and do not lean (my part) on your own understanding. In all your ways acknowledge (my part) Him, and He will make your paths straight (God's part) (Proverbs 3:5-6).

• **Acknowledge.** One of Joe Montana's greatest strengths was his ability to read defenses. Joe's arm strength wasn't the best–especially toward the end of his career. But his ability to recognize defenses was superior to any other quarterback that has played the game.

In this verse, acknowledge literally means to "recognize" God's presence and control. It's the idea of turning every area of life over to God. Jesus put it this way, "But seek first his kingdom and his righteousness, and all these things will be given to you as well" (Matthew 6:33). Have you acknowledged or recognized God in every area of your life? Don't leave God out of any decision you make.

• **Make Straight.** Few offensive lineman have received more attention than the '95 Nebraska Cornhuskers. Nick-named the "pipeline," they opened huge holes against the defense. No one was more appreciative of their efforts than the running backs. In many cases, all the backs needed to do was run straight through the path their 300-pound blockers opened.

When Proverbs refers to "make straight" it's the thought of making something smooth, straight or right. It's the idea of removing obstacles that are in the way. You can depend on the Lord to clear the way and smooth out our part.

God's program for stress relief involves pausing to pray. Take a step back from your circumstance and realize that God is ready to help you. "God says, 'Be quiet and still, and know that I am God" (Psalm 46:10 NCV). Then pray and tell God how you feel. "I pour out my problems to Him; I tell Him my troubles. when I am afraid, you, Lord, know the way out" (Psalm 142:2-3 NCV).

God's stress management program is simple. Bring your decision or circumstance to Him; look to the Bible as your playbook; and then follow God's coaching. The Master Coach will make your paths straight by both guiding and protecting you.

Unlike jury, athletes and fans divided about O.J. verdict

Sports celebrities and fans around the nation reacted to O.J. Simpson's acquittal Tuesday—some with relief, some with indignation. After the not guilty verdict in the trial, one prominent quarterback said, "There was tension in our locker room, and it wasn't good." A similar atmosphere pervaded other NFL teams, and, not surprisingly, feelings about the verdict were split along racial lines. In Dallas the day before the verdict, Cowboy tackle Nate Newton—as considerate, cooperative and engaging a personality as there is in the league—spoke aloud what many African-American players were feeling. "It doesn't matter if he's innocent or guilty," Newton said of Simpson to a white reporter. "It's not going to change what's going on in this country. You people have controlled us forever, and you'll continue to go on controlling us. That's just the way it is."

Most of the country either heard or watched the Simpson acquittal. And it was hard for whites to understand those blacks who cheered and celebrated the verdict. On the other hand, it was hard to figure the whites that stood dazed, shaken and angry as they listened to the verdict. The contrast between how whites and blacks reacted to the verdict was extreme–to say the least. Three-quarter of whites disagreed with the verdict, while that same number of blacks said justice was done.

It's difficult to understand how blacks and whites can see things so differently. Georgetown University Law School's Paul Rothstein tried to answer the different attitudes between blacks and whites, "Whites have had an unrealistic view of how perfect things function. Minorities probably have had an unrealistic view of how badly they function."

I've waited until I watched the "Million Man March" led by Louis Farrakhan before I finished writing this devotion on race relationships. And again, as I suspected, there seemed to clearly be different views between blacks and whites on the purpose and need for a day of atonement for black men. While many black men felt it was their obligation to be a part of this movement, regardless of Louis Farrakhan's controversial views on race relationships. Many whites failed to grasp why anyone would follow someone like Farrakhan whom they believe represents hatred and racism.

So what's the answer to bringing the races together? The success of the civil rights movement brought us integration—but more than 20 years later we still have problems between blacks and whites. Farrakhan and others have suggested a return to segregation. Neither integration nor segregation seem to be the answer that our society so desperately seeks. It's difficult to legislate people's attitudes. Changing laws does not change hearts. The civil rights movement served an important purpose in our history, but it's done about all that it can do to bring harmony between races.

Ultimately, the answer for racial tension is found in the Bible. Reconciliation, not integration nor segregation, is the answer. Unger's Bible Dictionary defines reconciliation as, "restoration to friendship and fellowship after estrangement. Old Testament reconciliation contains the idea of an atonement or covering for sin. In the New Testament it possesses the idea 'to change thoroughly from one position to another.' Therefore, it means to be completely altered and adjusted to a required standard."

The Bible can be divided into two categories: people and their relationship to God, and people and their relationships with each other. Once Adam and Eve had broken their fellowship with God by eating the forbidden fruit and Cain killed Abel, the remainder of the Bible deals with God's attempt to reconcile the human race back to himself and and to reconcile us to each other. Paul put it this way, "All this is from God, who reconciled us to himself through Christ and gave us the ministry of reconciliation: that God was reconciling the world to himself in Christ, not counting men's sins against them" (2 Corinthians 5:18-19).

Once blacks and whites are reconciled to God, then and only then, can the process of true racial harmony and understanding begin to take place. As always, society's answers to social problems must contain a spiritual component or we will continue to be divided.

Bulls' gamble: Add wild joker to pair of aces

Dennis Rodman sporting black-and-white fingernails and red hair emblazoned with a black Chicago Bulls emblem, is ready to go to work. "Why run off to the circus when the circus comes to you?" Coach Phil Jackson said Thursday on the eve of training camp. "We're going to see a lot of unusual behavior in Chicago." Phil Jackson is a practicing intellectual, an original thinker who has studied psychology, philosophy and religion most of his life. That might be an unusual background for an NBA coach, but it also could give the Chicago Bulls' mentor the edge he needs to understand the inimitable world of Dennis Rodman. The normally conservative Bulls have changed their stripes by acquiring the eccentric Rodman from the San Antonio Spurs, and they're gambling he will bring them a title and not turmoil.

Did the Chicago Bulls acquire a new mascot or the league's best rebounding power forward? Early in training camp, Rodman has already made some divisive comments about his new teammates. "They shoot a lot. They shoot too much, and nobody has really talked to me. That's fine with me. I'm in my own world out there," Rodman said.

Do you remember Dennis Rodman's defiant attitude he carried into last year's playoffs? During one playoff game the entire Spur's team huddled up during a time out, while Rodman sat at the end of the bench stretched out with his shoes off. While this act alone probably didn't destroy the Spurs opportunity to win the game, it was certainly symbolic of Rodman's defiant attitude.

Rodman made the cover of Sports Illustrated because of his defiant attitude. It's not just the sportsworld that has to deal with defiance. You can see examples of defiance in our culture's music, movies and schools. Madonna has made millions of dollars on CD's and videos from this same attitude. And prime-time TV shows no lack of defiant kids who challenge and their parents on sitcoms. None of this should take us by surprise. The Bible predicted that these acts of rebellion and stubbornness would happen "in the last days" (2 Timothy 3:1-2).

How does God view defiance? In the Bible, we read about King Saul who did his own thing, just as much as Rodman or Madonna do their own thing. God had provided instruction through the prophet-judge Samuel, but Saul chose to defy God's will. When Samuel confronted Saul about his defiance toward God, he told him, "For rebellion is as bad as the sin of witchcraft, and stubbornness is as bad as worshipping idols" (1 Samuel 15:23a, TLB). It's pretty obvious from this analogy that God doesn't think too much of a stubborn or rebellious attitude.

It's not only the unbeliever that struggles with defiance, but also believers. And it's not something that happens suddenly. Whether it's the parable of the prodigal son or examples from King Solomon's own life, the progression of defiance seems to follow the same pattern: compromise, followed by wild living and an unwillingness to be accountable to anyone else. Ultimately, King Solomon's defiant attitude toward God and the Scriptures led him to be turned off to spiritual things. He defied God by marrying a lot of foreign women who eventually turned his heart away from God.

What happens when we choose to defy God? Here is a statement made by Lord Byron many years ago, that still applies today: "The thorns which I have reap'd are of the tree I planted; they have torn me, and I bleed. I should have known what fruit would spring from such a seed." God uses the thorns that grow from our life to prick us back on the right path. Since He misses the close fellowship He had with us and wishes to regain it, He may discipline us. To defy God is to guarantee a miserable life. "The way of the treacherous is hard" (Proverbs 13:15b).

Recently, a coach I know chose to defy God by becoming involved in an immoral relationship. Their excuse was, "That's just the way I am. God made me this way." We should never forget that there are consequences for our actions. And we should be careful we don't try to rationalize our behavior or we can count on God taking action toward our defiance. And that's a gamble none of us should take.

The Curses of Rocky & The Bambino

Get real. "The Curse of the Bambino" and "The Curse of Rocky Colavito" have no place in serious baseball analysis. Double plays count. Double whammies don't. But if you're hung up on black cats, broken mirrors and the haunted tales of the Boston Red Sox and Cleveland Indians, take heed. These curses might be on a collision course in the American League playoffs. "It's kind of like the planets aligning. Which curse gives way first?" says author and Indians fan Terry Pluto, whose 13th book is "The Curse of Rocky Colavito." Will Cleveland, mired in mediocrity after trading power hitting young Rocco Demenico Colavito in 1960, go gloriously beyond its runaway division title? Will Boston escape the near-miss frustration it's known since selling Babe Ruth to the New York Yankees in 1920?

Superstitious fans or athletes are nothing new to sports. Some major league players won't step on the white lines or wear socks. A few get really weird like Wendell Turk. If he's not pitching without his socks, he'll chew licorice and brush his teeth in the dugout. Or he might draw three crosses in the dirt on the back of the pitching mound, then lick the dirt off his fingers. Unfortunately, all these silly curses and superstitions do is discount the supernatural world to many people. There really is a spiritual war going on, but it has nothing to do with superstitious curses or odd behavior. And although you can't see or hear it–it is real!

"Finally, be strong in the Lord and his mighty power. Put on the full armor of God so that you can take your stand against the devil's schemes. For our struggle is not against flesh and blood, but against the rulers, against the authorities, against the powers of this dark world and against the spiritual forces of evil in the heavenly realms" (Ephesians 6:10-12). Many Christians are unaware that there is a spiritual battle going on. While they worry about who will win the World Series or how their favorite player will perform, they fail to realize that there's a spiritual contest going on with life-and-death consequences.

What would be the chance for a batter to get a hit against a major league pitcher if he were wearing a blindfold? Not good. Nor does it make any sense to be unaware of Satan's strategies. This spiritual contest may be invisible, but both sides are playing for keeps.

Satan is no silly superstition. He might want you to believe he is no more real than the Easter Bunny, but believe me–he is both real and dangerous. Any team preparing for a game must first study their opponent. How well do you know the enemy? Here is a brief scouting report: First, Satan is an angel who was thrown out of heaven because he rebelled against God's authority (Isaiah 14:12-14). Second, he wants to not only beat you, but wipe you out. "Your enemy the devil prowls around like a roaring lion looking for someone to devour" (1 Peter 5:8). Finally, Satan met his match in the person of Jesus Christ. "Since the children have flesh and blood, he too shared in their humanity so that by his death he might destroy him who holds the power of death–that is, the devil–and free those who all their lives were held in slavery by their fear of death" (Hebrews 2:14-15).

A few years ago, Thurman Thomas couldn't locate his football helmet during a game. There was a lot of confusion and scrambling as everyone tried to find it. Equipment doesn't do us much good unless we wear it. Are you wearing the equipment that God has provided?

According to Ephesians 6:13-17, we should put on our spiritual equipment each day.

- "The belt of truth"–Be honest and faithful. Keep your commitments.
- "The breastplate of righteousness"–Live a godly and righteous life.
- "Feet fitted with...the gospel of peace"–Share the gospel with others.
- "The shield of faith"–Trust God for your security and strength against Satan.
- "The helmet of salvation"–This provides confidence for the battle.
- "The sword of the Spirit, which is the word of God"–Our only offensive weapon. Use it!

We face a powerful team of demonic forces whose goal is to defeat the church. We need to rely on God's equipment and direction to obtain the victory!

'Sandberg to return to baseball'

Ryne Sandberg, the All-Star second baseman who abruptly retired from the Chicago Cubs in the middle of the 1994 season, will come back and play in the major leagues in 1996, The Associated Press learned Monday. Sandberg was placed on the voluntarily retired list by the Cubs on June 13, 1994, after his sudden retirement from the Cubs at age 34. But the 10-time All-Star, considered one of the best all-around second basemen in the game's history will return next season at 36. Sandberg joins Michael Jordan as the second famous Chicago athlete who wore uniform No. 23 to unretire. Like Jordan, Sandberg decided he'd been away too long from a sport he always loved.

Just as everyone looked forward to Michael Jordan's return in Chicago, we had Sandberg's return to celebrate. Remember when Jordan returned to basketball? When he temporarily took a new number, 45, fans bought so many jerseys that there was a world-wide shortage of the material his jerseys were manufactured from. With Sandberg, it's not only the city of Chicago that looks forward to his return, but anyone who is a baseball fan. He not only makes the Cubs a more exciting team but he also brings something special to all of baseball.

For Christians there should be just as much eagerness about the return of Jesus Christ, as there is for the superstar athletes we watch. With Jordan and Sandberg, we could only hope that they would reconsider retirement and return to the sport they loved. But for Christians we know for a fact that Jesus Christ will return for those who love him.

"Look, he is coming with the clouds, and every eye will see him, even those who pierced him; and all the peoples of the earth will mourn because of him. So shall it be! Amen" (Revelation 1:7).

John's words in the book of Revelation read like a press release. He is announcing the return of Jesus to earth. Talk about good ratings! Everyone will see him arrive and they will know it is Jesus. And while we may eagerly await the amazing athletic feats by Sandberg, nothing compares to what Jesus will accomplish when he conquers evil and judges all people according to their deeds (Mark 20:11-15).

The return of Christ is often referred to as "The Second Coming." And it's no minor issue in the Bible. God's Word mentions the return of Christ or the end of time every 30 verses. Only 4 of of 27 New Testament books fail to mention Christ's return.

While Sandberg's return was determined by the baseball schedule, Christ's return can't be certain. The Bible says, "Now brothers, about times and dates we do not need to write you, for you know very well that the day of the Lord will come like a thief in the night" (1 Thessalonians 5:1-2).

No one can accurately predict the date of Christ's return, so it's foolish to try and pinpoint the exact day. While Christians often disagree about what events will lead up to the return of Christ, there is little disagreement about what will happen once Christ does return:

1. Christ will return visibly with a loud command.
2. There will be a clear and understandable cry from an angel.
3. There will a trumpet fanfare that is unequaled in history.
4. Believers in Christ who are dead will rise from the grave.
5. Believers in Christ who are alive will be caught up in the clouds to meet Jesus.

Since the Lord's return will be unexpected, we should be ready at all times for His return. Suppose He were to return today. How would He find you living? Are you ready for His return? Shouldn't we live each day as if Christ were going to return anytime?

While we might disagree on when Christ is coming back—one headline is for sure: 'Christ to return to earth.' Are you ready?

Panthers shock 'Niners 13-7

Less than 10 months after reigning as Super Bowl XXIX champions, the battered San Francisco 49ers plummeted to new depths at 3Com Park Sunday. Never mind Dallas. The 49ers became the first defending Super Bowl champion to lose to an expansion team. "We're playing like an average team," center Jesse Sapolu said in a shocked 49ers locker room afterward. "We got beat by an expansion team, and that shouldn't happen to us. This is about as low as we can get."

In just a few short months, the San Francisco 49ers went from the penthouse to the outhouse. Well not quite. But their record dropped to 5-4. That's something that seemed improbable when the season started. After all, after crushing the Chargers in the Super Bowl, this team was labeled as perhaps the greatest in 49er history.

Even an expansion team has discovered the 49er's Achilles heal. If you remember your Greek mythology, Achilles was the son of Peleus, King of the Myrmidons, and Thetis, a sea goddess. Achilles was considered the bravest and most handsome warrior in the army. During his childhood he was dipped into the magical waters of the river Styx. Every part of his body that touched the water became invulnerable. Only his heal was untouched by the water. That's where we get the term, "Achilles' heal."

While the fall of the 49ers may be premature, there can be no doubt that other teams have discovered an Achilles' heel. For the 49ers their Achilles' heel has been an injury to star quarterback Steve Young. Other injuries and key off-season trades have only made them more vulnerable to opposing teams.

Each of us has our own Achilles' heal. For some, it's pride; for others, money. For Samson it was sensuality. He's the Bible's

Superman. He killed a lion with his bare hands and later beat a thousand-man army with only the jawbone of a donkey. But even Superman is vulnerable to something. For Superman it was kryptonite, for Samson it was his lustful, desire for women.

For the San Francisco 49ers it's pretty obvious that their weakness involves the loss of key players. But many of us are like Samson when it comes to vulnerability in our relationship with God—we have a blind spot. What is your Achilles' heel? Is it anger . . . worry . . . greed . . . alcohol . . . drugs . . . selfishness . . . lust . . . pride? Here are a few lessons from the life of Samson (see Judges 13-15):

• **Surround yourself with friends that will help you identify any blind spots in your life.** "Faithful are the wounds of a friend, but deceitful are the kisses of an enemy" (Proverbs 27:6). A friend has your best interests at heart and will give you advice that is for your own good. An enemy, by contrast, may say nice things that you want to hear, but may ruin your life.

• **Know the source of your strength.** Samson didn't see God as the real source of his strength. Instead, he saw only his own strength (see Judges 15:14-17). God allowed Samson's strength to be taken away so he would learn that he was weak without God's power. Don't become dependent upon your own talents and abilities. Otherwise, you may find God teaching you a painful lesson about leaning on Him, rather than yourself. Do you depend on God for your security, strength and safety?

• **God can help you overcome past defeats.** Even though God had disciplined Samson for blowing it, God still came to his aid when he reached out. Samson said, "O Lord God, please remember me . . . . " (Judges 16:28). Although you may feel like God has forgotten you, He never forgets you. In spite of samson's past failure, God still answered his prayer and destroyed the pagan temple.

Don't let your Achilles' heel defeat you. Instead of being shocked and blindsided by your weakness, let God provide the power to help you reach your potential.

Heisman race: Multiple-choice question (Teamwork, Part 1)

Some Heisman Trophy candidates—Leeland McElroy, Stephen Davis, Lawrence Phillips—have come and gone. More, it seems, have stayed. One month before college football's most prestigious award is handed out, the race remains unusually unsettled. Nebraska's quarterback Tommie Frazier has surged into a favorite's role in recent weeks, and Ohio State Tailback Eddie George has gotten there with steady performances. But at least a dozen players figure to get regional support. At least one former winner wonders about the fuss. "I was thinking," Florida coach Steve Spurrier says, "how come they don't talk about who's going to be the MVP in the NFL all year long? Everybody just talks about trying to get to the playoffs; they don't have to worry about who's voting for who, and nobody has to promote themselves. Individual awards are nice. But team championships are much, much more rewarding."

Spurrier is right. Team awards can be much more rewarding than individual rewards. It's a matter of putting the emphasis on the team, rather than the individual. Most coaches believe that a team can't reach their potential without putting the emphasis on the team, rather than a few individuals. The Bible also has a lot to say about teamwork, rather than self-promotion. For the next three devotions we'll examine acrostic (T-E-A-M) on the key characteristics of teamwork.

Time Together. You can't develop relationships between the members of the team, unless they spend time together. You can see the problem each year in the NBA when they play the All-Star game. Throwing together the best players in the league doesn't necessarily guarantee the best team performances. Since their practice time is limited, you rarely see the kind of teamwork that is part of the regular season. Many of the greatest teams in sports history have been veteran teams like the Steelers in football, the Celtics in basketball and the Yankees in baseball.

Jesus spent three years with his disciples. Their cohesiveness and team spirit wouldn't have been possible without the time they spent together. The result of their teamwork impacted history. No team has ever had a greater impact on the world than Jesus Christ and his disciples. Time together is part of what makes a team successful. But it's also what you do during that time that brings a team together. Here are a couple of important characteristics of successful teams:

• *Trust.* Trust is the emotional glue that holds a team together. When you can depend upon your teammates to do their part then you can put all your energies into your job. Mistrust causes others to slow down or move cautiously through their task. The only way to build trust among teammates is to act consistently. The early church had to trust one another as it began to expand its influence. "Paul and Barnabas appointed elders for them in each church and, with prayer and fasting, committed them to the Lord, in whom they had put their trust" (Acts 14:23).

• *Patience.* Every member of a team needs patience. Sometimes it's needed by the players who sit on the bench. Other times it's the more experienced members of the team that need to be patient with the less experienced members as they learn the system. And always there is the need to listen patiently to the coach or other teammates as they share their ideas. When we talk too much and listen too little, we communicate to others that we don't think too much of their ideas. "Everyone should be quick to listen, slow to speak and slow to become angry" (James 1:19).

• *Love.* The Bible often talks about a love that is very different from what many call love in our society. Real love is not lust. Unlike lust, God's kind of love is directed outward toward others, not inward toward ourselves—it's unselfish! And most importantly God's kind of love is not based upon conditions. Fans love teams and athletes—if they win. But if they hit a losing streak—forget it. That kind of love is based upon a set of conditions. God's love is unconditional. During the '95 National Championship football game, Nebraska's All-American offensive guard Zach Weigert told his teammates that regardless of the outcome of the game, he would still love them. That's unconditional love. The Apostle Paul defines love in 1 Corinthians chapter 13, then he encourages us to just do it in the next chapter.

Chiefs winning without legendary Montana (Teamwork, Part 2)

With all due respect to the great Joe Montana, who needs him? Not the Kansas City Chiefs, who stand atop the NFL with a 9-1 record in Montana's first year of retirement. "Joe did a lot for this team," wide receiver Willie Davis said. "But I think a lot of people here just sat around and waited and thought if the game was close, Joe would find a way to save us. We didn't play as a team. Now we're playing as a team." The Chiefs were 19-10 in Montana's two years. "It wasn't Joe's fault. It was our fault," tackle-tight end Joe Valerio said. " What happened is this team went, 'Ok, Joe, you're the best quarterback ever. Go out and win this game for us.' Well, Joe is the best quarterback ever; nobody is saying he's not. But we put all the pressure on Joe, and we weren't playing as a team."

I find it interesting that the 49ers apparently never lost sight of the importance of teamwork. Maybe it was that Joe started his career in San Francisco, so there wasn't a perception that he should be able to win games on his own. Whether it's Joe Montana or Michael Jordan, without teamwork no team can reach its potential. Previously we examined the first part of our **T-E-A-M** acrostic: Time spent together. As we continue our look at teamwork, here are the next two characteristics:

Encourage your teammates. The Apostle Paul knew how important it was not only to be encouraged by his teammates but to be an encouragement to them. "Paul sent for the disciples and, after encouraging them, said good-by and set out for Macedonia. He traveled through that area, speaking many words of encouragement to the people..." (Acts 20:1,2). While you may not have as much talent to offer your team, encouragement is something everyone can offer. We all need to be an encourager. Paul said, "Therefore encourage one another and build each other up" (1 Thessalonians 5:11).

What you say to a teammate does affect their attitude. And if you affect their attitude you've affected the behavior of the entire team. If the Apostle Paul were your coach, here is what he might say, "Do not let any unwholesome talk come out of your mouths, but only what is helpful for building others up according to their needs, that it may benefit those who listen" (Ephesians 4:29). There is little doubt that positive feedback builds up and improves athletic performance. That's why most teams prefer to play at home. When 80,000 screaming fans are yelling, "Go for it!" it's pretty hard to give less than your best effort.

Here are few suggestions on how to encourage your teammates:

• A word of encouragement. Call out their name if they make a good play. If they blow it—reassure them that it's only temporary. Be as specific and natural as you can. You don't need to flatter them—just be honest. Let your teammates know that you appreciate them. "Oil and perfume make the heart glad, so a man's counsel is sweet to his friend" (Proverbs 27:9).

• High-five, hug or handshake. Any appropriate, physical acknowledgment will be appreciated.

• A warm smile. Don't fake it! Be yourself, but don't walk around with a frown on your face. "When a king's face brightens, it means life; his favor is like a rain cloud in spring" (Proverbs 16:15).

Assist your teammates. There are at least two ways you can assist your teammates.

• Play your role on the team. When the ministry of Jesus was becoming more popular than that of John the Baptist, rather than being jealous of Jesus, John said, "He must become greater; I must become less" (John 3:30). John understood his role was to support Jesus by helping prepare the way for Jesus' ministry.

• Look our for the best interest of your teammates. Since selfish ambition, vain conceit, and self-centeredness tear down team unity, looking out for your teammates' interest brings unity. The unselfish athlete doesn't use words like, "I," "me," and "mine." Humility is what makes this possible. "In humility, consider others better than yourselves. Each of you should look not only to your own interests, but also to the interests of others" (Philippians 2:3,4) We'll finish our T-E-A-M acrostic next time.

Maverick Personalities hobble Dallas (Teamwork Part 3)

Put Dallas' renaissance on hold, at least until Jimmy Jackson and Jamal Mashburn realize they're on the same team. They deny a drift, but they aren't in sync. Neither are the Mavs, 6-9 following a recent seven-game slide. Enough is enough, says Coach Dick Motta: "There are a couple of people who got mad at each other, and they've paralyzed our team. They won't pass to each other; they won't speak to each other. They're being very immature about it. I won't be embarrassed anymore. I told the players those loud cracks they hear are the ankles of people jumping off the bandwagon. I've always said the only thing that could hurt the Three J's (Jimmy Jackson, Jamal Mashburn and Jason Kidd) is if the fourth J became 'jealousy.'" Says Mashburn: "If anyone has personal agendas, they are hidden. All I know is we got the same players, we're not the same team."

In the last two devotions we examined the first part of our T-E-A-M acrostic: T - Time spent together, E - Encourage your Teammates, and A - Assist your Teammates. As we continue our look at teamwork, here is our final look at the characteristics.

Maintain Team Spirit. As Coach Dick Motta found out, maintaining team spirit is not easy. And the more talented the team, the more likely they may be faced with what Motta calls the fourth J - "jealousy." So how can a team maintain team spirit? It begins with each of the members of team following a couple of basic fundamentals of teamwork.

• Respect for your coach (leader). Respect for authority is critical to team spirit. Without a chain-of-command concept of authority, there is confusion and chaos. The chain-of-command is a biblical concept that God gives us so we can function properly. For the Mavericks, the chain-of-command is the head coach followed by the assistant coaches and then the players.

In 1 Peter it says, "Servants be submissive to your masters with all respect . . . for this finds favor with God" (1 Peter 2:18-20). It may be difficult to respect a coach or leader who doesn't appear to deserve your respect, but you are responsible to follow their lead. Your attitude toward him or her will greatly impact how your team works together.

• Forgive and forget your teammates' mistakes. Everybody blows it sooner or later. Even the most talented athletes are prone to mistakes. If you have any doubts, take a look at the NFL blooper films. These films show professional athletes who run the wrong way, drop simple passes and fall on their faces. If a pro athlete can make mistakes, so can your teammates. "Let all bitterness and wrath and anger and clamor and slander be put away from you, along with all malice. And be kind to one another, tender-hearted, forgiving each other, just as God in Christ also has forgiven you" (Ephesians 4:31-32).

In addition to forgiving, it's also important to forget. Don't fume about a teammate's mistake. The Bible says, "Lord, how many times shall I forgive my brother when he sins against me? Up to seven times?' Jesus answered, 'I tell you not seven times, but seventy-seven times" (Matthew 18:21-22).

Forgetting means:

1) Refusing to keep track of their mistakes.

2) Don't keep score (1 Cor. 13:5).

3) Be bigger than the offense (Psalm 119:165).

4) Refuse to hold onto any judgmental attitude (Matt. 7:1-5).

The power of teamwork can improve any team's performance. A team of athletes working together can accomplish much more than the separate members working individually. That's what "synergy" is. The word synergy means that "the sum total is greater than the total separate parts." It's the idea of working together. Some experts have estimated that if you could get all the muscles in your body to pull in one direction, you could lift over 25 tons. In Buckminster Fuller's book, Synergetics, he says, "One plus one can equal four if we put our efforts together in the same direction." Commit yourself to making your efforts equal more by pulling in the same direction as the rest of the team.

Titlists return, rejoice, reflect

The range of Tom Osborne's emotions about winning a second consecutive national college football championship was as complete as his team's 62-24 Fiesta Bowl victory over Florida. "It was a terrible year and it was a great year," the Nebraska head coach told a press conference at the Tempe (Ariz.) Mission Palms Hotel. "It was taxing. It was gratifying to work with a group of players with that focus and drive, and that is the saving, redeeming factor." Osborne called this year's team his best team ever. But the Huskers' 1995 season, despite a 25-game winning streak and back-to-back national titles, was surrounded by controversy.

So much in sports depends on your vantage point. As Coach Osborne faced a season filled with adversity and success, his perspective helped to determine his attitude.

Perspective is how we view something. The term suggests the idea of "looking through . . . seeing clearly." Like most people in America, I watched the Fiesta Bowl match-up between Nebraska and Florida. But my perspective was different from most fans–I was on the sidelines taking photographs. As I took pictures, I was constantly trying to keep my camera properly focused on the action. At times I was focused on the wrong players and my pictures were worthless. Once, during Tommie Frazier's quarterback sneak for a touchdown, I ran out of film. Yet another time, I shot a picture of Lawrence Phillips flipping into the end zone for a touchdown–but I cut off his legs in the picture. Occasionally, I would take a picture that was sharp and properly focused on the action.

What is true of my experience taking photographs is true of sports and life. And Tom Osborne is a good example of someone who kept both in perspective during the 1995 championship season.

A few years ago, a shoe company used the slogan "Life is short, play hard" to sell its sneakers. That's not a bad perspective for athletes. But even a better slogan for the Christian athlete would be "Life is short, pray hard." Using this slogan, let's think about what we can learn from God's Word and Coach Osborne's season.

LIFE IS SHORT. Listen to how the Bible makes this point in Psalm 90 . . . like yesterday when it passes by (v. 4a) . . . like grass . . . it sprouts and withers (vv. 5-6) . . . like a sigh (v. 9) . . . soon it is gone . . . (v. 10) Later in the Bible, James says, "What is your life? You are a mist that appears for a little while and then vanishes" (James 4:14). Since life is so brief, how should we view the present? During the press conference with Tom Osborne following the championship game he went on to say, "I learned a lot this year. I take my spiritual life very seriously and there were some times when I ran on empty and relied on my spiritual life."

We can waste our time and energy on what's wrong in life or we can focus on the redeeming factors in life. "Consider it pure joy, my brothers, whenever you face trials of many kinds, because you know that the testing of your faith develops perseverance" (James 1:2,3). The Bible is clear—life is too short to waste time reflecting on our negative circumstances.

PRAY HARD. One lesson I learned at the Fiesta Bowl about taking pictures was the right lens makes the photographer. Without the proper capacity to zoom-in on a play or receive the proper amount of light, you can forget taking good pictures. If you want to scope in on the big picture in life, then you'll need a lens that includes prayer and the Bible. Prior to the national championship game, Coach Tom Osborne quoted 2 Timothy 1:7 to his team, "For God did not give us a spirit of timidity," the apostle Paul wrote to Timothy, "but a spirit of power, of love and of self discipline." While many coaches might be leading their team in a rah-rah victory speech, Coach Osborne was quietly letting his team know where he was coming from. And where he was coming from is a life spent in devotion to God. Life is short, pray hard!

Wuerffel has a 'spiritual calm'

"I have a saying, "Do your best and forget the rest," Danny's father Jon
Wuerffel said. "The Lord is the ultimate person who decides if you're
going to get up from that hit or if the ball is going to be caught. You have
to finally turn things over to the Lord. That's where Danny gets what I
call his spiritual calm." Wuerffel's high school coach and now Gators
offensive line coach, Jimmy Ray Stephens, says, "There is no question
his spiritual depth is the thing that gives him that poise and composure."
Before a Fellowship of Christian Athletes Fiesta Bowl breakfast for 1,200
on Thursday, Wuerffel took exception with Nebraska receivers coach Ron
Brown, who compared God to a thrower. "I think of God like the offensive line. He keeps you safe and protected."

Florida's quarterback Danny Wuerffel realizes how important
his spiritual calm is to his athletic success. Fear is perhaps the
greatest barrier to achieving athletic success. But it's not just
excelling at a sport that strikes fear into our hearts. What is it in
your life? Death? Disaster? Disease? What are the things that
frighten you the most?

What effect do our fears have on us? First, fear limits our
success and keeps us from reaching our potential. Fear often creates
what it fears. The Bible says, "Above all else, guard your heart, for
it is the wellspring of life" (Proverbs 4:23). In this passage, Solomon
is warning us to be careful about what we think because our lives
are shaped by our thoughts. If we focus on what we fear then it's
more likely that what we fear will happen in our lives.

Second, fear destroys our relationships. If we always fear
rejection, then it's likely that we'll never develop the type of
relationships that God wants for us. Whether it's the relationships
within our family, or a small group of men or women who support
and hold us accountable, the relationships will not grow deep
without the absence of fear.

So what's the answer to conquering our fears? The Bible teaches that we should turn our fears into prayers. "I sought the Lord, and he answered me; he delivered me from all my fears" (Psalm 34:4). David describes in Psalm 27 a time when he was cornered by his enemies. He had every reason to believe that because he had been rejected by others that he had failed and should quit. But God hadn't rejected David and he knew that if his confidence was in the Lord, he could overcome his fears. "The Lord is my light and my salvation . . . The Lord is the stronghold of my life . . . Though an army besiege me, my heart will not fear; though war break out against me, even then I will be confident" (Psalm 27:1,3). God is clear—freedom from fear begins with a relationship with Him: "So do not fear, for I am with you; do not be dismayed, for I am your God. I will strengthen you and help you; I will uphold you with my righteous right hand" (Isaiah 41:10).

The Apostle Paul offers the same advice: "Do not be anxious about anything, but in everything, by prayer and petition, with thanksgiving, present your requests to God. And the peace of God, which transcends all understanding, will guard your hearts and your minds in Christ Jesus" (Philippians 4:6,7). A famous sportswear company uses the slogan "No Fear" on its shirts. If we want this slogan to be more than words on our chest, then we'll need to worry less and pray more! Whenever we start to feel our lives being gripped by fear, we should turn to God.

God's spiritual calm doesn't come from positive thinking, absence of conflict, or in feeling good about ourselves. It's knowing God and believing He is in control of our lives. God may be like a thrower, but I also agree with Wuerffel. God is like the perfect offensive line. No sacks. No hurries. No penalties. He will keep us safe and protected—you can count on it.

White determined to not let attack on church alter focus

While preparing for the biggest game of his 11-year NFL career, Green Bay Packers defensive end Reggie White has had his attention diverted from football to arson to racism. White's church—the Inner City Community Church in Knoxville, Tenn.—was set ablaze Monday, and racial epithets were left at the scene. "All of this hate, racism and ill will, all it has done is made me more determined in my game and in my message to get out on and off the football field. And that's what I'm going to do, regardless of the hate."

Reggie White can probably identify with the battle between David and Goliath.

First, both David and Reggie faced giants. David's was a champion from Gath who was over nine feet tall and wore a coat of scale armor that weighed about 125 pounds. White, an ordained minister, faces both racial epithets and physical harm. He was told Friday night that his church had received a message that something was going to happen. "They said the caller told them he was tired of these interracial churches and marriages and schools and that he was going to do something about it. He said he was upset over the bank we opened in Knoxville to help people empower themselves, though it helps whites as well as blacks. So, since it happened three days after the call, somebody had the arson planned all along." White went on to explain, "There are six other interracial and black churches in the state of Tennessee that have been burned recently and this has been happening in recent weeks from states from California to Tennessee. At our site, some skinhead material was found there."

Second, both David and Reggie faced an opponent that had backed everyone down. Goliath taunted Israel's soldiers with his impressive size. And even their leader, Saul, may have been especially worried because he was the best match for Goliath. But in God's eyes Goliath was no different from anyone else. Racism is a problem that has backed down many leaders. Racial hatred is a social problem in our country today that appears to be unbeatable. White was asked if he is afraid that harm may be done to his family—wife, Sara, son Jeremy (9) and daughter, Jecolia (7). "No, I am not. I know what God can do and I know what he wants me to do. And they cannot tear that down with words, hate or even fire."

Reggie knows what David knew when he faced his giant. Goliath had a big advantage against David from a human standpoint. But Goliath failed to realize that in fighting David, he also had to fight God. David announced to Goliath, "You come against me with sword and spear and javelin, but I come against you in the name of the Lord Almighty, the God of the armies of Israel, whom you have defied. This day the Lord will hand you over to me, and I'll strike you down and cut off your head. Today I will give the carcasses of the Philistine army to the birds of the air and the beasts of the earth, and the whole world will know that there is a God in Israel" (1 Samuel 17:45, 46).

Neither Reggie nor David waited for everyone else to join the battle. Criticism couldn't slow them down. And each decided that there was no reason to wait. By doing what was right in God's eyes, they were pleasing the One whose opinion matters most. White now wonders when the rest of God's people will join him in the battle against racism. "When is America going to stop tolerating these groups? It is time for us to come together and to fight it. One of the problems is that the people financing and providing the resources for this type of activity are popular people with money who are hiding under the rug. Some of them may be policemen, doctors, lawyers, prominent people who speak out of both sides of their mouths."

Isn't it about time the rest of us on the sidelines joined the battle with Reggie? Whose opinion matters most to you? Is it the crowd around you or the Lord Almighty that David turned to for strength when he faced a giant? The people of Israel saw Goliath as too big to hit, but David saw a giant that was too big to miss. There's no secret strategy to defeat racism in America. We need to speak out against hatred and begin to show genuine concern for others. We need to stop talking about loving our neighbor and start doing it.

Players let four-letter words fly

Well, nobody is saying parents concerned about objectionable programs should get V-chips to block out TV sports. But in two NFL games Sunday, four players used profanities in live postgame network TV interviews. NBC analyst Paul Maguire says we need to consider the motive. "These people are very excited. I don't think anything was done intentionally to embarrass or hurt anybody. I think they didn't even realize they said something offensive." But he should have, says NBC analyst Phil Simms, who'll work the Super Bowl with Maguire. "It bothered a lot of people. I've been there. I know it's such an emotional game. But you have to know you're talking to an audience when they stick out a microphone. You can't let that happen. And it's absolutely the obligation of the players—you do owe something to the public."

Talk. The airwaves are full of it. Whether it's radio talk shows or cable sports shows, it's everywhere. And the more we talk, the more likely it is that we will say something we shouldn't. Take the case of one player who let a four-letter word fly. Michael Irvin of the Cowboys insists that he will say what he wants whenever he wants. His mom says not so fast. "I will be talking with my boy," Pearl Irvin said from her home. "I don't need to tell you he didn't learn to speak that way in this house. I told all my kids act ugly and the world will treat you that way. If he hasn't remembered that, maybe I'll have to pass it on again, too" While Irvin may avoid a spanking, you can bet he won't avoid a scolding.

Obscenity's overuse is on the rise. And while its use has been common in many locker rooms over the years, its recent overuse in public has dampened its shock value. Like many other offensive behaviors in society, obscenity is normally associated with humor; so we gradually become more tolerant of it. Former Education Secretary William Bennett, crusading to clean up daytime TV, watched the two NFL games with his sons. He said the incidents show swearing is "in the mainstream. Now it's over the doggone airwaves." It's not "the end of the world, that three jocks use dirty language," he said. "It's one more notch . . . Civilizations don't collapse all at once, they do it one degree at a time." Christians are not always exempt from the problem of profanity or misuse of the tongue: far too often they contribute to it. Here are some warnings from the Bible about the tongue:

"The tongue that brings healing is a tree of life, but a deceitful tongue crushes the spirit" (Proverbs 15:4).

"Those whose teeth are swords and whose jaws are set with knives to devour the poor from the earth, the needy from among mankind" (Proverbs 30:14).

Keep in mind that it's not really the tongue that's the message's source. No, the source of the profanity is the heart. "The mouth speaks out of that which fills the heart" (Matthew 12:34). Since the heart is the problem, here are some suggestions for muzzling the tongue.

• **Think before you Speak.** It's a common saying, "God gave you two ears and one mouth, so listen twice as much as you speak." Emotion is no excuse for letting a few choice four-letter words fly. Athletes need to apply the same self-control used during the game to their postgame interviews. James put it this way: "My dear brothers, take note of this: Everyone should be quick to listen, slow to speak and slow to become angry" (James 1:19). David prayed, "Set a guard over my mouth, O Lord; keep watch over the door of my lips" (Psalm 141:3).

• **Self-control begins with memorizing God's Word.** David's strategy for controlling the tongue will work for us today. "I have hidden your word in my heart that I might not sin against you" (Psalm 119:11). James called the tongue a deadly poison and an untamed beast. Want to keep from being flagged for obscenities? Memorize and apply God's Word to your situation. Like pick-and-roll in basketball, it's a simple strategy, but difficult to apply. But as my basketball coach used to say, "Perfect practice, makes perfect."

Magic looks sharp in first game back

After 4 1/2 seasons of retirement and stints as a coach and owner, Magic Johnson checked back in to the NBA on Tuesday night. Wearing a uniform so new it still had wrinkles and his new "MVP" shoes were flown in specially from Taiwan. Johnson couldn't contain his enthusiasm for the game he was forced out of when he contracted the virus that causes AIDS. The 36-year-old star shed his warmups and took the court with less than three minutes gone in the Lakers' game with Golden State. He was on the floor when the final buzzer sounded, just two rebounds shy of a triple-double. Johnson finished with 19 points,10 assists and eight rebounds in 27 minutes as Los Angeles defeated the Warriors 128-118.

It was just another amazing comeback! His stats for his first game back were even better than Michael Jordan's on his return to the NBA. Most of us who rooted for George Foreman's unlikely comeback also cheered Magic on his return to the NBA. Our society loves underdogs and comebacks. It's why many find sports exciting and interesting.

As I thought about Magic's desire to return to basketball, I wondered why anyone in his situation would be motivated to come back. After all, in his first go-around he made plenty of money and received more recognition than nearly any player before him. He did most of the things others can only dream about. And though he said his return was partly so his 3-year-old son could see him play, I think there were probably a few more reasons for risking a comeback at his age. What motivates athletes? There are at least three basic philosophies for motivation that apply to any athlete. Let's examine each.

• **Recognition (Psychological).** The desire for power and prestige motivates many athletes to excel. There is often a sense of power or status from athletic achievement. Some athletes have a strong desire for personal awards or achievement, while still others may be motivated toward team goals. While recognition is a strong motivational force, it depends on circumstances. It's often difficult to control the factors that lead to power or status. Someone who plays on a team that has a lack of talent, has little hope for winning the championship or gaining much attention. And this motivation doesn't always explain why athletes act the way they do. If recognition works all the time, then why do so many powerful achievers still feel unsatisfied?

• **Physical pain and pleasure (Physical).** Many coaches believe that nothing would get done without their athletes either seeking pleasure or avoiding pain. Examples of this type of motivation are anger, fear, or financial reward. It might be a threat of running sprints or doing pushups, but in each case the athlete responds to the pressure to seek pleasure or avoid pain. Many athletes will do almost anything to avoid a scolding from a coach–but this type of motivational force doesn't explain all behavior. And it's not always clear which athletes will respond to a particular reward or punishment.

• **Service to God (Spiritual).** Athletes have a psychological dimension, physical dimension, and spiritual dimension. Each of these dimensions can motivate us to excel. But both the psychological and physical factors often depend on circumstances. You may not always play on the team with the best talent, or possibly you don't respond to intimidation tactics. Here is God's principle for motivation: Devotion to God for the development and exercise of Christian character. It's the only acceptable motive for actions that are pleasing to God. Many other factors that motivate us are self-centered, such as money or fame. Our devotion to God should be motivated by our love for Him. The Apostle Paul taught us to express our love for God through our physical abilities, which include your athletic performance. He wrote, "Therefore, I urge you, brothers, in view of God's mercy, to offer your bodies as living sacrifices, holy and pleasing to God–this is your spiritual act of worship" (Romans 12:1). Because God loves us, and because He gave his Son to make our new lives possible, we should joyfully give ourselves as living sacrifices for His service.

Hard work secret of brothers' success

Meet basketball's fabulous Barry boys, four brothers whose famous father, Rick, won NCAA and NBA scoring titles. Scooter, Jon, Brent and Drew Barry are the sons everyone supposes were born with a golden touch in the tips of their tiny fingers. "If my boys were racehorses," Rick has said jokingly, "they'd be worth millions on bloodlines alone." Indeed, all four play at basketball's highest levels, each a late bloomer who earned a scholarship. But hard work rather than heredity is the real secret to their success. "Believe me, the jump shot is not hereditary," says Scooter, 29, who plays professionally in Germany. "If my last name wasn't Barry, you'd never compare my game to my dad's."

It's common in sports to find many father and son combinations. In baseball there's Bobby and his son Barry Bonds. In football there's Archie and Peyton Manning. And of course, in basketball there are the Barrys. In each case fans have high expectations because of what the fathers accomplished in their careers. But a bloodline is no guarantee of success. Hank Aaron, the greatest home run hitter of all-time, son's career never took off. He struggled through several years in the Braves minor league system before his father encouraged him to retire.

Since hereditary is not necessarily a guarantee of future success, than how can we predict someone's ability to succeed? I think Scooter Barry's point about his jump shot not being hereditary is part of the answer. Hard work and training are probably better determining factors of future success in sports than heredity. That's not to completely disregard a person's bloodline, but without training you can't succeed.

What's true in sports, is also true in our spiritual lives. God commands us to be constantly training ourselves toward godliness. Although you may have been raised by godly parents, their influence through training you to be godly had much more to do with your character development than your bloodline.

The Apostle Paul didn't take his spiritual son, Timothy's, godliness for granted. Although Timothy was his teammate for many years, Paul thought it was necessary to encourage him to train himself to be godly. "Have nothing to do with godless myths and old wive's tales: rather, train yourself to be godly." (1 Tim. 4:7).

When Paul instructed Timothy to train himself in godliness, he used a familiar term to athletes and coaches. The verb that some Bible's translate as "exercise," "train," or "discipline," originally referred to athletes who competed in the sports of their day. Later the word "train" meant the training or disciplining of either the body or the mind in a skill. For us to understand how to train ourselves to be godly, we need to understand three basic questions:

• **Who is responsible for my training?** (Train yourself). Paul said, "Train yourself." Of course none of us can grow spiritually without God's help, but Paul's point was that Timothy must work or pursue his training. God was certainly at work in his life, but we can't be lazy in our approach to spiritual growth. No Olympic athlete can afford to simply relax their training schedule a few weeks before their event. Neither can we pray, "Lord, make me a godly," and expect God to instantly turn us into some spiritual giant.

• **What is the goal of my training?** (Devotion to God). Paul also reminds Timothy that the goal for training himself for godliness was growth in his personal life, not his ministry. Paul had instructed Timothy earlier to be concerned with the growth of his ministry, but here Paul wants Timothy to be concerned with his own devotion to God. Paul's instruction to Timothy is a good reminder for us. We should be more concerned with personal devotion to God, rather than our amount of Christian activity.

• **What do we need to train properly?**
  • Use the right equipment (Bible).
  • Practice godliness (No short-cuts).
  • Learn from a personal trainer (Be discipled by godly men and women).

Morrison sends message

Half an hour after a phone call confirmed the worst—that a second round of tests found him HIV-positive—an emotional Tommy Morrison climbed atop a podium Thursday and offered himself as a warning. "I ask that you no longer see me as a role model," said the 27-year-old boxer, "but see me as an individual who had an opportunity to be a role model and blew it. Blew it with irresponsibility, irrational, immature decisions . . . that one day will cost me my life."

Morrison sent a clear message—"I blew it!" He didn't make excuses for his immoral behavior; not even a hint of shifting the blame to his upbringing or substance abuse—just confession. Morrison's statement is refreshing, to finally see an athlete stand up and honestly admit his guilt. But Morrison isn't the first person to send this type of message to the world about sin and confession.

First let's define sin. It's not a word that we use every day, though we see it in the lives of ourselves and others like Tommy Morrison. The word "sin" is an archery term. It means "missing the mark." The "sin-mark" is the distance between the bulls-eye on a target and the place the arrow hits. When the Bible says we have sinned, it's describing our missing the mark of God's perfection. It's falling short of His glory. Sin offends our holy God and separates us from Him. Just as oil cannot mix with water, sin cannot mix with God.

Now that we have defined "sin," let's think about the message God sent about the consequences of sin sent through His messenger Isaiah. "But your iniquities have separated you from your God; your sins have hidden His face from you, so that He will not hear" (Isa. 59:2). Now let's examine God's view of sin.

• **Sin cannot be ignored.** Many in our society turn their back on sin, hoping not to notice the damage it does or the offense it is to a holy God. Experts often argue about kids being desensitized to violence by watching too much television. Is it possible that Christians have become desensitized toward sin? Because we watch it on TV, see it at the movies, or hear about it in the locker room, have we gotten to the point of turning our back on sin? Jesus didn't ignore sin. In fact, as the Pharisees discovered, Jesus confronted their pride and selfish-ambition. "Woe to you, teachers of the law and Pharisees, you hypocrites! You clean the outside of the cup and dish, but inside they are full of greed and self-indulgence" (Matthew 23:25).

• **Sin cannot be excused.** We live in a society that has turned nearly everyone into a victim. It's no longer just the person who was violated by the crime, but now it's also the violator who has become the victim. That's why I appreciated Morrison's remarks at his press conference. He didn't try to excuse or blame his behavior on other people or circumstances. Jesus didn't excuse the righteous when they neglected to help the poor. "They also will answer, 'Lord, when did we see you hungry or thirsty or a stranger or needing clothes or sick or in prison, and did not help you?' He will reply, "I tell you the truth, whatever you did not do for one of the least of these, you did not do for me." Then they will go away to eternal punishment, but the righteous to eternal life" (Matthew 25:44-46).

• **Sin cannot be tolerated.** Perhaps the only view in our society that is not tolerated is no-tolerance. The only person not tolerated is often the person who believes in moral absolutes. When the money changers in the temple interfered with worshiping God, Jesus wouldn't tolerate their sin so he went on the offensive by clearing the temple of their presence.

One day the HIV-virus will cost Morrison his life. But the bigger issue is, will Morrison allow his sin to separate him from a holy God? It's one thing to lose your life to AIDS, it's quite another to be eternally separated from God. Morrison's one eternal hope is to not only confess the sin in his life, but to also confess Jesus Christ as Lord and Savior.

Gooden: Out of darkness

Dwight Gooden found his guardian angel at a Narcotics Anonymous meeting in St. Petersburg, Fla., last June. At the time, Gooden, once the most feared pitcher in baseball, was serving a one-year suspension for violating his drug and alcohol aftercare program. He was working out at a local college, throwing pitches from a shabby mound on a torn-up field. Gooden had a broken spirit and a lost soul. After a week of listening to other addicts talk about the difficulty of their recoveries, Gooden approached Dock, an ex-Marine who became hooked on drugs while in Vietnam, and asked if he'd be willing to be his "sponsor" to teach him the Twelve Step program and help him learn to stay clean one day at a time. "Are you serious about turning your life around?" inquired Dock. "I need a second chance at life," Gooden insisted. Since that moment eight months ago, Gooden hasn't gone a day without meeting with or speaking to Dock. "I've looked death in the eye many times. Just being here now is a miracle. . . I'm not going to blow it." Adds Dock: "Dwight has a spirituality that he never had before. He's not measuring himself in baseball terms. He's doing it in life terms. There's an inner peace."

Dwight Gooden's struggle is to stay sober one day at a time. But you don't have to be addicted to drugs to face difficult choices in life. Like Dwight, many Christians must choose which road they will follow. Dwight's friend, Dock, puts it this way: "I worry about him on the road. It's only natural. He's going back into life in a new way–clean and sober–and it'll be different." However, Gooden won't allow himself to forget the road he has traveled, and Dock constantly reminds him this is one playing field he won't graduate from.

As I watched CBS's coverage of the Final Four, I thought about the theme they open each show with, "The Road to the Final Four." They've used a similar theme for the college football national championship, as well. For Dwight Gooden, or any of us, the theme could be "The Road to Eternal Life." You see, each of us too will choose daily which road to travel. Which road will you choose? The Fellowship of Christian Athletes' has developed a model for challenging athletes to take the high road. I've tied their One Way 2 Play–Drug Free! program into this idea of taking the high road.

Faith in Jesus Christ (High Road versus Low Road). First, let's define the high road. For the Christian, the high road involves faithfully choosing God's way instead of man's way. Faith doesn't mean we disconnect our brains and ignore our responsibility to think. Instead, it's the idea of recognizing that each of us has a limited ability to think and reason. The Bible puts it this way, "As the heavens are higher than the earth, so are my ways higher than your ways and my thoughts than your thoughts" (Isaiah 55:9). That's why we need to study God's playbook, the Bible. Without God's direction, each of us is limited to our own understanding. This was Solomon's point when he wrote, "Trust in the Lord with all your heart and lean not on your own understanding; in all your ways acknowledge him, and he will make your paths straight" (Proverbs 3:5,6). Of course, none of us can lean on God's wisdom without first trusting in Jesus Christ for our salvation. It's only through a relationship with the living God that we can choose the high road.

Commitment to say "no" to alcohol and other drugs (Take the High Road). There's no way to stick with a commitment or steer clear of problem areas without God's power. Recognize that you can't do it on your own. Only God can provide the power! "But you will receive power when the Holy Spirit comes on you; and you will be my witnesses in Jerusalem, and in all Judea and Samaria, and to the ends of the earth" (Acts 1:8). The person who flip-flops between God's way and their own wisdom is called double minded in James 1:8.

Accountability to one another (Help to stay on the high road). Once you're part of God's team, then you need to be accountable to your teammates. No quarterback can run the option without the cooperation of his line. "Two are better than one, because they have a good return for their work: If one falls down, his friend can help him up. But pity the man who falls and has no one to help him up!" (Ecclesiastes 4:9-10).

State Stunned by death of ex-Husker Quarterback

Brook Berringer, the backup quarterback who helped Nebraska win the 1994 national title, was killed Thursday when the small plane he was piloting crashed in a farm field. Berringer was 7-0 as a starter during the 1994 season when Tommie Frazier was sidelined with blood clots in his leg. He played sparingly behind Frazier last season when Nebraska won its second straight national title with a 62-24 rout over Florida in the Fiesta Bowl. Berringer had been scheduled to speak at the Fellowship of Christian Athletes banquet at the Devaney Center in Lincoln, where people and players at the dinner hugged one another. "Brook would want this event to go on as planned," Nebraska coach Tom Osborne, told the banquet audience. "I know he would want it to be done in the spirit with which it was intended to honor God. Brook honored God. Brook enjoyed life to the fullest."

I was shocked. Only a few hours had passed since Brook's plane crashed when I heard about his death at the FCA banquet. I was so surprised I don't even remember who told me the news. Any death is tragic, yet whenever a young person suddenly dies it's hard to accept.

Most Nebraska football fans knew Brook. However, only a few people outside the state knew much about Brook besides what they saw on the football field. I think it's important for me to reflect on what we should all know about Brook Berringer.

At the FCA Banquet Coach Osborne said, "If you had somebody that you wanted your son to be like it would be Brook. He was just a good guy. He was one of those people who stood for all the right things."

Two of Brook's former teammates, who spoke at the FCA banquet, talked about Brook. Aaron Graham, a team co-captain at center, said, "We lost a great person who was a great friend." Tony Veland, a senior safety said, "Brook was a great teammate, a great friend and a great person. All his teammates are hurting."

Brook was obviously a great player and person. But most important of all he was a Christian. Only a few short months ago he made a decision that changed not only his life, but his destiny. Art Lindsay, who spoke for Brook at the banquet, shared how Brook committed his life to Christ.

"I met Brook several years ago when I heard his name mentioned at the football stadium. I had never heard of him before, but for some reason the Lord placed it on my heart to pray for him. During the next several years we became good friends. This past August, I asked him if he had ever put his faith in Jesus Christ. When he asked me what that meant, I told him. I shared that God's Son Jesus came to earth and died for each of us so we might have eternal life. I asked him if he wanted to take that step of faith by placing his trust in Jesus Christ. He explained that he had never understood what people meant by a relationship with Christ. But now that he understood it. He wanted this relationship for himself. We prayed together and Brook joined God's team. During the past few months we spent much time together praying and studying the Bible. When I asked him where he wanted to be in five years, he responded by telling me that he only cared about growing closer to Jesus Christ in this newly found spiritual relationship. There was no mention of the upcoming NFL draft or which team he might like to play on. Clearly Brook had become a child of God."

Brook's untimely death is a wake-up call for all of us. Salvation is the single most important decision in life. Yet, if we are not careful, we'll put it off. Fortunately, Brook didn't delay his decision to accept Jesus Christ as Lord and Savior of his life. Take a moment to read the following Scriptures. Don't postpone making the same decision.

1. We are lost (Romans 3:10-18).
2. We are sinful (Romans 3:23).
3. We need God's help (Romans 6:23).
4. Christ died for us (John 3:16).
5. Heaven is available (John 14:1-3).

When Brook Berringer joined the Nebraska football team, he became a hero for thousands of fans. And while most fans will remember him as a part of the back-to-back national championship teams, I'll remember him as my teammate in Christ. "Therefore, if anyone is in Christ, he is a new creation; the old has gone, the new has come!" (2 Corinthians 5:17).

Don't mess with the refs

Los Angeles Lakers point guard Nick Van Exel's seven-game suspension and NBA-record $25,000 fine for shoving a referee sends a clear message to players. The league won't tolerate its officials being abused. "I think everybody understands if this happens again, the penalty will be even more severe," NBA vice president, operations Rod Thorn said. Van Exel's suspension, the third-longest in league history for an on-court incident, comes three weeks after Chicago's Dennis Rodman was suspended for six games and fined $20,000 for head-butting referee Ted Bernhardt. Rodman also kicked over a water cooler and shouted obscenities.

Little more than a week later, Van Exel's teammate Magic Johnson, was ejected for bumping an official during a game with the Mavericks. Many fans were surprised and upset by Johnson's actions. Even Magic Johnson admitted, "It's really bothering me. I try to do the right things and set examples for the young players—not just on our team but all young players." While some fans were not surprised by Rodman's headbutt of an official, it came as a shock to most that cool-headed Magic Johnson would mess with an official just days after preaching to one of his own teammates about self-control.

Thomas Jefferson suggested a way to handle anger in his Rules of Living, "When angry, count ten before you speak; If very angry, a hundred." Another author, Mark Twain. "When angry, count four. When very angry, swear." Unfortunately, because some of today's NBA players lack the ability to control their anger their actions have become more severe than simply words.

How can we overcome anger? Whenever our anger is based on selfishness or wrong motives it becomes sin. Here are several practical ways to deal with your anger.

• **Understand why you get angry.** Most of the time, anger is based on selfishness. Think about it. Why does a baseball player throw his bat in disgust after he strikes out? What ticks off a basketball player when an official's call goes against him? How about a football player that's benched for making a mistake during the game? Usually, anger is motivated by frustration, insecurity and personal injury. Recognize the source of your anger and realize that it's wrong. "A man's wisdom gives him patience" (Proverbs 19:11).

• **Stop and think before reacting.** Most athletes would guess that the leg muscle is their most powerful muscle. However, it's the muscle in their mouth that can do the most damage and is the most difficult to control. Van Exel received his second technical foul for calling referee Ron Garretson "a little midget." Learning to keep the tongue in check will literally turn away wrath. "A gentle answer turns away wrath, but a harsh word stirs up anger" (Proverbs 15:1). And as Johnson, Van Exel and Rodman can attest to: a lack of self-control can be trouble. "He who guards his mouth and his tongue, guards his soul from troubles" (Proverbs 21:23).

• **Overlook petty disagreements.** No doubt that referees in the NBA may need to do a better job of dealing with players' tantrums, but most of the blame falls on the players. Reasonable people simply do not attack referees for receiving a technical foul. It's hard to believe someone is a victim when they're shoving a referee over a table. "The beginning of strife is like letting out water, so abandon the quarrel before it breaks out" (Proverbs 17:14).

• **Don't hangout with angry people.** While it's not practical to avoid contact with a teammate who is prone to temper-tantrums, it is possible to limit your time around them or others with this problem. If you hang around people who are angry, you know what happens. You become angry and negative. "Do not associate with a man given to anger; or go with a hot-tempered man, lest you learn his ways, And find a snare for yourself" (Proverbs 22:24,25).

Public Enemy No. 1

The most reviled man in baseball stood in the jubilant visiting clubhouse at Jacobs Field last Saturday and cried like a baby. They were not tears of joy because his Baltimore Orioles had advanced to the American League Championship Series by knocking off the heavily favored Cleveland Indians. They were tears of regret about what happened on Sept. 27, when he became so enraged that he spit at umpire John Hirschbeck, and then was vilified from coast to coast. Roberto Alomar told Sports Illustrated at his locker, "I'm not a bad person. I care about my family. I care about my kids. I'm from a good family. I made a mistake. God knows I didn't mean anything bad."

The response to Alomar's behavior was swift and harsh. Whether an outburst is verbal or takes the form of spitting or an obscene gesture–it's wrong. However, it's important to realize that no athlete is perfect. Roberto Alomar is a reminder of this fact. To friends, teammates and his coaches, Alomar's outburst was a surprise. Teammate Mark Parent said, "He's not a monster. He doesn't have a rap sheet. I've known him and his family since he was 17. He's a nice kid from a great family. His parents taught him the right and wrong way. Now people think he's Ty Cobb." If an athlete never offends in word or deed he is a perfect man or woman. Obviously, none of us qualifies–not even a good kid like Roberto Alomar.

So how can a major mistake be overcome? In 1 Samuel 12, the prophet Samuel gives us a game plan for getting back on track after we've blown it.

• **God will not give up on you.** *Sports Illustrated* reported Alomar's problems with this headline, "Public Enemy No. 1." Their article went on to explain fan reaction to Alomar's blunder. "He was booed every time he came to the plate and was routinely subjected to the kind of abuse directed at him last Friday, after he struck out in the third inning of Game 3: Four fans raced to the seats behind the Orioles' dugout, screamed at and taunted Alomar, and then high-fived each other." In 1 Samuel 12, the prophet Samuel explained that although the nation of Israel had blown it by selfishly asking God for a king, rather than relying on Him as their king, God had not given up on them. "Do not be afraid," Samuel replied. "You have done all this evil; yet do not turn away from the Lord, but serve the Lord with all your heart" (1 Samuel 12:20). God will never abandon us, even when others turn their backs on us.

• **You haven't blown it so badly that God can't forgive you.** "For the sake of his great name the Lord will not reject his people, because the Lord was pleased to make you his own" (1 Samuel 12:22). Will people forgive Roberto Alomar for spitting in an umpire's face? One teammate, Brady Anderson, responded to this question by saying, "As time goes on, I think so. When they see how remorseful he is, how much he wants to atone." While others might make us Public Enemy No. 1, we serve a God that showed his love and mercy toward us even while we were still sinners. "But God demonstrates his own love for us in this: While we were still sinners, Christ died for us" (Romans 5:8).

• **Stop doing what is wrong and start doing what is right.** Samuel told the nation of Israel to turn away from the evil that they had done and begin serving God. It's never too late to start doing what is right. Three days after Alomar spit on Hirschbeck he issued a public apology and pledged $50,000 to a foundation that fights a rare disease that Hirschbeck's son died of in 1993. Let's hope Brady Anderson is right and Alomar is remorseful and will atone for his mistake by doing what is right. "He who conceals his sins does not prosper, but whoever confesses and renounces them finds mercy" (Proverbs 28:13).

• **Focus on the future and remember God's promises.** It won't be easy for Robert Alomar to keep his focus on baseball under this cloud of controversy and intimidation. But despite our circumstances, God promises to be with us. It may not mean that our circumstances will change, but at least we can face them with the proper focus. "But those who hope in the Lord will renew their strength. They will soar on wings like eagles; they will run and not grow weary, they will walk and not be faint" (Isaiah 40:31).